GRADE 5

Grammar and Writing Handbook

ISBN: 0–328–07541–8

3 4 5 6 7 8 9 10 V000 09 08 07 06 05 04

scottforesman.com

Editorial Offices: Glenview, Illinois • Parsippany, New Jersey • New York, New York
Sales Offices: Parsippany, New Jersey • Duluth, Georgia • Glenview, Illinois
Coppell, Texas • Ontario, California • Mesa, Arizona

TABLE OF CONTENTS

Writer's Guide

Ideas and Content

A good writer develops a plan before writing. The writer needs a **main idea** and a **purpose.** The main idea is the point the writer wants to make. The purpose is the reason for writing. For instance, the purpose of some writing is to inform with facts. Other writing is meant to persuade, using convincing ideas, or simply to entertain with an interesting story.

When you prepare to write, first consider possible topics. Choose the one that interests you the most. Then decide whether you want to inform, persuade, or entertain your audience. Write possible main ideas, and let your ideas flow as you plan. Don't be afraid to change your mind. Select the main idea that makes the most sense as you consider who your audience is.

List **details** that fit your topic and support your main idea. Add interesting information that will appeal to your audience. Now decide which details are the strongest.

Look at the following example, which shows the plans of one writer who has listed details and then eliminated the weakest ones.

Main Idea: Persuade Mom to adopt a dog

Details:

Will teach me responsibility
Will play with me
Promise to walk it every day
I saw cute dog in park

Will keep me company
Some dogs fluffy
Will take care of it

> **FOCUS**
>
> **Check that the details you use support your main idea. Eliminate details that are off the subject or weak.**

Strategies for Choosing a Topic and Purpose

- Choose a topic that you will enjoy writing about. If you care about your topic, you will be able to write with enthusiasm.
- If you cannot think of many supporting details, change your main idea.

A Match the number of each writing assignment below with the letter of the purpose that best suits it.

> **A** To entertain   **B** To inform   **C** To persuade

1. A summary of a speech you heard
2. A funny story about a silly squirrel
3. A recommendation to buy a certain book
4. A humorous description of a mistake you made
5. An essay about how to shoot a basketball

B Read the paragraph below. Write the numbers of the sentences that do not support the main idea in the first sentence.

6. I think I can learn to ride a snowboard if I develop my skills and use my experience. **7.** In order to succeed, I will need good balance, good concentration, and patience. **8.** My English teacher knows that patience is good when I make a mistake. **9.** If I fall down, I just need to get back up again. **10.** Basketball players have really good balance. **11.** I already know how to ski, so I can apply similar techniques to learn how to ride a snowboard.

C Read the chart below. The topic is the President of the United States. Write a sentence stating your own main idea about the President based on any three of the details. Then write a sentence about each detail you have chosen, to complete a four-sentence paragraph.

Main Idea: _____

Details: Leader of the United States
Signs bills passed by Congress into law
Commander-in-Chief of Armed Forces
Discusses problems with world leaders
Chooses other important officials

Organization

When you write, put your ideas in an order that will help readers understand them. **Organization**—the structure, or the way ideas are put together—allows writers to show the connections among those ideas.

Here are examples of ways you can organize your writing to help readers understand the points you want to communicate:

- as a story, from beginning to middle to end
- as a comparison/contrast essay, describing likenesses and differences
- as a persuasive argument, expressing one convincing reason after another
- as a how-to report that clearly presents a series of steps

When you begin writing, pay attention to how you organize each paragraph. Each sentence should express a complete idea. The sentences in a paragraph should fit together and appear in an order that makes sense. Use words that help a reader see how ideas are related. For example, one sentence can pose a question, and the next sentence can begin to answer it.

Organize your paragraphs too. The ideas in each paragraph should flow from the information in earlier paragraphs.

Strategies for Organizing Ideas

- Tell events in the order in which they happened, from first to last.
- Begin a paragraph with a topic sentence that expresses the main idea, and then write details that support the main idea.
- Use order words (*first, then, after, finally*) so your writing flows smoothly.

GRAPHIC ORGANIZER

Use a graphic organizer to help you organize your ideas. For example, consider creating a web, a Venn diagram, an outline, or even a quick sketch.

A Match the number of each writing assignment with the letter of the organization it calls for.

A Story   **C** Persuasive Argument

B Comparison/Contrast   **D** How-to Report

1. Describe the similarities and differences between a poem and a play.
2. Tell about an imaginary grasshopper with super powers.
3. Explain how to play baseball.
4. Convince someone to make a donation to a local charity.

B Rearrange the order of sentences in the paragraph below so that the sentences flow smoothly from one to the other. Write the new paragraph.

5. The giraffe and the frog began to talk. **6.** Then one day a giraffe stooped way down and noticed the frog. **7.** "Oh!" said the giraffe. "I had never noticed you before." **8.** He would sit all alone on his lily pad and watch the animals play. **9.** As they chatted, the two became best friends, and the frog was no longer lonely. **10.** Once upon a time there was a lonely frog that had no friends.

C Use order words to complete the how-to paragraph below. Then write two sentences of your own to end the paragraph.

11. _____ choose the cereal you like best.
12. _____ open the box.
13. _____ pour the cereal in a bowl.
14. _____
15. _____

Writing Organization   **9**

Voice

Good writers usually have a strong **voice** that comes through in the tone and style of their writing. A strong voice will help to make your writing interesting by showing your personality.

- Today began nicely. I felt happy. (weak voice)
- Today I leaped out of bed with a big smile on my face. (strong voice)

When you write—just as when you speak—you can choose an appropriate tone of voice to communicate successfully with a certain audience for a particular purpose. Your style and your choice of words can make the writing interesting to each reader, whether the tone is serious or humorous, formal or informal. If you care about what you write, your writing will reflect your voice.

Strategies for Developing Your Voice

VOICE
Use the pronoun *I*, along with vivid adjectives *(nervous, excited, cautious)*, to express how you feel about something.

- Choose a writing tone that matches your topic. For instance, a light, carefree tone probably would not work for writing an essay about your state's government. Instead, you would need to use a more formal, serious tone.

- Use words and phrases that match the type of writing you are doing. For example, in a letter to the editor of your local newspaper, you should avoid using slang or casual language. In a letter to a friend, however, you would use informal and friendly words. In this type of writing, you could even use slang.

- Find your voice by reading aloud things you have written. In other words, learn to listen to yourself.

A Match each numbered item with the type of writing it is.

    A Personal Narrative   **C** Persuasive Argument
    B Humorous Description   **D** Comparison/Contrast Essay

    1. Elephants may be big, but whales are even bigger.
    2. I believe that all schools should be free.
    3. The scruffy toy bear had been hugged flatter than a raggedy pancake!
    4. I was overjoyed when Cassandra slid into her chair beside me.

B Each underlined part of the following paragraph has a "voice problem." Match the letter of the problem with each numbered item.

    A Slang   **B** Too informal   **C** Too formal

    5. My school is <u>way huge</u> compared to any other school in the city. **6.** In such a large school, I can <u>make the acquaintance of</u> many different people. **7.** However, classes are large, and students might receive less attention <u>(as if they really cared)</u>.

C Add descriptive words or phrases to the sentences to express a strong, lively voice.

    8. I went to the airport and saw _____ airplanes. **9.** When the airplanes took off, they made such a loud sound that _____. **10.** I met a _____ pilot who told me what it was like to _____. **11.** Seeing a plane in flight makes me feel _____.

Word Choice

Good writers choose their **words** carefully. They use specific words to make their meaning clear. They also use vivid words to add excitement to their writing. Look below to see how the writer's word choice makes the sentence lively.

- Nat threw the ball to the batter. (dull)
- Nat grunted as he hurled a curve ball to the batter. (lively)

Strategies for Improving Word Choice

- Use exact nouns. (*hotel* instead of *place, oil painting* instead of *picture)*
- Use strong verbs. (*flinch* instead of *move, barked* instead of *said)*
- Use vivid adjectives. (*tattered* instead of *old, drenched* instead of *wet)*
- Avoid vague words such as *great, nice, thing,* and *stuff.* ("I smell roses" instead of "I smell things")
- Create strong images to make your readers use their senses. ("Gillian's face turned red as a tomato" instead of "Gillian was embarrassed")
- Decide if some sentences that have linking verbs would be stronger with action verbs. ("My heart thumped" instead of "I was excited")
- Avoid wordiness. ("I think we will win the game because we have better players" instead of "In my opinion, I think we will win the game due to the fact that we have better players")

> **SYNONYMS**
>
> **Synonyms** are words that have similar meanings. Use a thesaurus to help you find vivid words to replace ordinary words.

A   Write the more vivid or exact word to complete each sentence.

1. Charlotte (jogged, went) along the winding path.
2. The breeze drifted through the (forest, place).
3. She (mumbled, spoke) to herself.
4. Then she noticed a (funny, squiggly) line in her path.
5. She stooped and realized that it was just a (thing, worm).

B   Write the letter of the word-choice strategy for each underlined word or words.

A Exact noun   **C** Strong verb
B Vivid adjective   **D** Sense image

6. Charlotte saw a beautiful <u>doe</u> at the edge of the woods. **7.** Suddenly, the deer <u>bounded</u> away.
8. When it ran into the woods, <u>its white tail flashed in the sunlight</u>. **9.** Charlotte was glad she had caught a glimpse of this <u>graceful</u> animal.

C   Replace the underlined word in each sentence with a more exact or vivid word. Write each word you choose.

10. Charlotte <u>was</u> on the path.
11. She heard animals <u>move</u> in the woods.
12. Suddenly, a huge gust of wind <u>went</u> through the forest.
13. Then Charlotte felt <u>the</u> raindrops on her face.
14. The clouds looked <u>bad</u>.
15. Lightning flashed, followed by a loud <u>noise</u>.
16. She put on her raincoat and <u>went</u> home.

Sentences

Good writers express their thoughts in lively, varied **sentences.** They make reading a pleasure by using sentences to create a special rhythm and style. Look at the short paragraph below. Note how the writer varies sentence type and length to make the writing interesting.

What should you keep in mind when adopting a dog? I think all dogs are wonderful, but some dogs are better than others for certain people. For instance, hunting dogs need a lot of exercise. Do not get a hunting dog if you can't take her for frequent long walks. Instead, think about adopting a small dog that needs less exercise. Enjoy your new pet!

Strategies for Improving Sentences

- Write sentences that flow logically from one to the other.
- Vary sentence length by including a mixture of short and long sentences.
- Avoid sentences that are too long or wordy. Think about rewriting one very long sentence as two or more shorter sentences.
- Avoid writing a series of short, choppy sentences. Use connectors such as *and, but, or, because, although,* and *however* to join two simple sentences.
- Include different kinds of sentences to add variety and life to your writing. Usually sentences will be statements. Sometimes questions, commands, or exclamations are good choices too.
- Try to vary the beginnings of your sentences. Avoid beginning all of your sentences with words such as *I, she, he, then,* or *the.*
- Read what you write aloud to yourself. Listen for a rhythm as if you are listening to a song. Rewrite sentences that interrupt the flow.

A Combine these short, choppy sentences. Use the connector provided. Add a comma if necessary. Write the sentences.

1. I like to collect stamps. They are interesting. *(because)*
2. Judy likes to paint. She is just a beginner. *(although)*
3. Some children collect toy cars. Other children collect dolls. *(and)*
4. My brother played with trains. I strummed a guitar. *(while)*
5. I like collecting baseball cards. I like playing baseball even more. *(but)*

B Each sentence in the following paragraph is too long. Rewrite each sentence as two or more sentences. Remember to begin each sentence with a capital letter and to use the correct end punctuation.

6. Last Saturday, my best friend, Eric, came over and we built a model car and then we painted it. 7. When it was time for lunch, we made sandwiches and drank some milk, and then we played baseball. 8. After baseball, we read and listened to music and then we talked about the next model car we wanted to build. 9. The afternoon flew by and when it was time to go home, we said goodbye and agreed to meet again next weekend. 10. I love having Eric over because we always have a good time and he is such a fine friend and I hope he will be my friend forever.

C Write a paragraph that describes your favorite hobby. Include at least one command and one question. Try to include a variety of long and short sentences.

Conventions

A **convention** is a rule that people agree to follow. Written language follows special conventions. For instance, sentences always begin with capital letters and end with some kind of punctuation. Sentences about the same topic are grouped together to form paragraphs. Conventions also set the rules for spelling and grammar. Look at the sentences below. How many conventions can you name?

- Greg Harding was born in Nashville, Tennessee, on March 3, 1996.
- He is a student at Griffin Elementary School, and his favorite classes are English and math.

Strategies for Conventions

- Learn the rules for spelling. For instance, add **-s** to form the plural of most nouns.
- Use a dictionary or spell-checker to help you with the spelling of difficult or new words.
- Capitalize the first letter of each word that begins a sentence.
- Capitalize the first letter of each important word in proper nouns.
- Use punctuation correctly.
- Make sure the verb you use agrees with its subject. ("I like Martin" instead of "I likes Martin")
- Check that the verb tenses are correct.
- Check that pronouns are used correctly in subjects and predicates.
- Make sure you use apostrophes correctly to show possession and to form contractions.

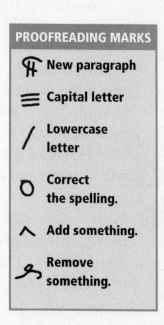

PROOFREADING MARKS

⸤	New paragraph
≡	Capital letter
/	Lowercase letter
○	Correct the spelling.
∧	Add something.
⸓	Remove something.

A Choose the correct word to complete each sentence. Write the word you choose for each sentence.

1. (greg, Greg) likes to complete his homework before dinner.
2. Then he likes to call (his, him) friends to chat.
3. Some of his friends (is, are) from the track team.
4. Some of (them, they) are very talented athletes.
5. A few of (Greg's, Gregs's) friends (do'nt, don't) like sports at all.

B Match the letter with the mistake in each sentence.

A Correct a misspelling.
B Capitalize proper nouns.
C Add correct end punctuation.
D Make the verb agree with its subject.
E Add an apostrophe.

> **PROOFREADING**
>
> **Always check your writing to make sure you use conventions properly.**

6. My best friends name is Robert. 7. Robert was born in Africa, but he moved to the united States when he was eight. 8. He is a fantastic soccer player 9. I are constantly amazed at the tricks he performs with a soccer ball. 10. Robert promised to teech me some of his tricks.

C Write five sentences about one of the topics below. Make sure you follow the conventions for proper spelling, grammar, punctuation, and capitalization.

- Your best friend
- Your favorite sport
- Your favorite class

Using a Scoring Rubric

How is *excellent* writing different from *good* writing? How do we know when writing is *not good?* One way to judge writing is by using a scoring **rubric.** A rubric is a checklist of *qualities,* or things to look for, in writing. See pages 6–17 for a discussion of these qualities.

Rubrics give a number score for each quality. You can use a rubric such as the one below to judge your writing.

SCORE	IDEAS/CONTENT	ORGANIZATION	VOICE	WORD CHOICE	SENTENCES	CONVENTIONS
4	Clear, focused, well-supported ideas	Smooth flow of ideas from beginning to end, with connecting words	Honest, engaging, lively writing	Precise, interesting, and accurate words	Smooth, varied, and rhythmic sentences	Excellent control with only minor errors
3	Ideas usually focused and supported	Information given in some order	At times reveals writer's personality	Correct and adequate words	Generally smooth, varied sentences	Good control; no serious errors prevent understanding
2	Ideas sometimes unfocused and undeveloped	Little direction from beginning to end	Fails to engage audience or show emotion	Limited vocabulary; lacks freshness	Awkward or wordy sentences with little variety	Weak control with errors that make writing hard to read
1	Ideas confusing and unsupported	Ideas hard to follow, with no direction	Flat writing with no feeling	Incorrect, dull, or overused words	Choppy sentences; run-ons or fragments; *and* overused as connector	Many errors that prevent understanding

Writing Models

Following are four responses to a prompt. Read the responses and the notes below them to see how each piece got its score.

Writing Prompt: Write about solving a difficult problem.

> When I was in first grade, I got lost in Biggie Mart. Go ahead, laugh. I know it's funny. When we were inside, I shot off to the game section. Later, I tried to find my grandma and got a little (I said a little, not a lot, OK?) scared. I dashed back to the toy place. I threw a fluffy blue sweater on the floor so I wouldn't pass it again. About two minutes later I saw the sweater again. I was going in circles. Now I began to panic. Maybe she left me! Suddenly I saw her investigating personalized mousepads in the computar section. I ran and gave her an enormus hug, and I suddenly felt very happy.

SCORE 4
Ideas/Content Focused on the problem; supported with details
Organization Time order signaled by *when, later,* and *now*
Voice Writer's personality reflected in strong voice
Word Choice Exact nouns *(Biggie Mart);* vivid adjectives *(fluffy blue);* strong verbs *(shot, dashed)*
Sentences Lively, varied sentences
Conventions Few mistakes; some misspellings *(computar, enormus)*

When I was eight, all of my friends were playing flag football. I wanted to play more than anything else. Finally, I got up my nerve and asked Coach Ori how do you play flag football? He said, "Well, first put two flags on each side of the field. Then you pick your team. You have to run hard to score a touchdown. Players are tagged instead of tackled. The team with the most touchdowns wins." I told him, "Thanks, coach." After that I felt happy because I could play. Now Im teaching my cousin Andy to play. He's talented and eager to learn.

SCORE 3

Ideas/Content Focused on the problem and supported with details

Organization Connectors such as *first* and *then* make events flow smoothly; ending somewhat weak

Voice Writer's feelings shown *(I felt happy…)*

Word Choice Lack of vivid verbs and nouns

Sentences Clear sentences with some variation

Conventions A misspelling *(Im)* and punctuation errors

One day I was in school. I did all my work. School finished and then it was after school. There were two of my friends in the after school. They always use to fight because I sat by one and the other one got mad. There names are Jackie and Yeselle. So it continued the same way. So the other day I was mad. So I had to tell them to stop fighting but they wouldn't. I solved it by sitting by myself every day. The next time I saw both of my friends they were very happy. Then I felt happy because they did'nt fight over me anymore.

SCORE 2
Ideas/Content Focused on the problem but lacks vivid details.
Organization Shows some order from beginning to end
Voice Writer's personality revealed
Word Choice Limited, dull word choice (*did, it, was, sat*)
Sentences Poor flow between sentences; some sentences confusing and wordy; a run-on sentence; many sentences beginning with *so*
Conventions Misspellings (*There* instead of *Their, did'nt*); poor grammar (*They always use to fight…* instead of *They always used to fight…*)

One time me and my friend's went to Rocky Grove amuzement park. We got on a ride. Then we got with his sister and his parents left us so me and him looked in all the rides then we found his brothers and their friend who were going on a ride called the american spirit so we went with them.

SCORE 1

Ideas/Content No explanation of what the problem was; missing important details

Organization Lacks organization; no clear ending

Voice Weak voice that does not reveal writer's personality

Word Choice Limited, dull word choice (*got*)

Sentences Awkward, run-on sentence; wordy and repetitive

Conventions Capitalization mistakes; misspelling (*amuzement*); pronoun errors; incorrect use of apostrophe (*friend's*)

Grammar and Writing Lessons

Sentences

A **sentence** is a group of words that expresses a complete thought. A sentence may be a statement, a question, a request or command, or an exclamation. All sentences begin with a capital letter and end with a punctuation mark.

Sentence: Jerry kept a journal.
Not a sentence: Kept a journal.

A Read each group of words. Write **S** if it is a sentence. Write **NS** if it is not a sentence.

1. Do you keep a notebook to record ideas?
2. Jerry enjoyed writing poems.
3. His poems about animal.
4. Do you know why Jerry kept a journal?
5. He stored his thoughts and feelings there.
6. Boxes of notes in a drawer.
7. Jerry shared his journal with his best friend.
8. Many famous writers publish their journals.

Choose the group of words in ( ) that will complete each sentence. Write the complete sentences.

9. _____ asked about our favorite inventions. (Our teacher, Never once)
10. My favorite invention _____. (the car, is electricity)
11. _____ makes it possible to run machines. (Out of power plants, Electrical power)
12. Each morning, people _____. (turn on lights, from all over the world)
13. Without electricity, many things _____. (could not be done, harder)
14. _____ is hard for me imagine. (Just imagine, A world without electricity)
15. Electricity _____. (life better than, makes our lives easier)

B Match each word group on the left with a word group on the right to make a sentence. Write each sentence.

1.	Can you	A	tried to invent something?
2.	A day without TV	B	work for years on an idea.
3.	Most inventors	C	are created in a day.
4.	A few inventions	D	imagine life without inventions?
5.	The Internet	E	would seem strange.
6.	My favorite invention	F	is a fantastic invention!
7.	Sometimes my dad	G	is the computer.
8.	With my computer, I	H	browse the Internet.
9.	Have you ever	I	uses my computer.
10.	For years, I	J	worked on a robot.

C Add a word or group of words to complete each sentence. Write the sentences.

11. My favorite invention _____.
12. This wonderful invention _____.
13. _____ didn't have this invention.
14. Years ago, they _____.
15. The most surprising thing _____.
16. _____ must be very hard to do.
17. _____ is a fairly recent invention too.
18. That clever device _____.
19. _____ use it very often.
20. A thoughtful inventor _____.
21. _____ will help anyone think about inventions.

Review and Assess

Read each group of words. Write **S** if it is a sentence. Write **NS** if it is not a sentence.

1. In the past twenty years, video games.
2. Some video games help pilots learn how to fly.
3. Video games in many countries.
4. Astronauts use similar types of games for training.
5. They learn about complex machines from the video games.

Read the following paragraph. Write the letter of the group of words that will make a complete sentence.

6. People with special needs _____. **7.** _____ give people who cannot walk the ability to move on their own. **8.** Special devices on some new traffic lights _____. **9.** _____ provide a signal for visually challenged people. **10.** A person with hearing loss _____. **11.** _____ really have helped improve people's lives.

6. A from inventions
   B many people
   C many inventions
   D benefit from inventions

7. A Wheelchairs, as one example,
   B When is it a
   C Either here or
   D Of the wheelchair

8. A or the other lights
   B in very busy traffic
   C make beeping noises
   D cars, buses, and trucks

9. A These beeps
   B Do you know
   C Sounds are
   D In several years,

10. A anywhere in the world
   B may wear a hearing aid
   C if a hearing aid
   D with an invention

11. A In so many ways,
   B Inventions such as these
   C All of a sudden
   D Doesn't it matter

Telling About *You* in Personal Narratives

A personal narrative tells about you and your experiences and feelings. Use details to make information and events clear and interesting. Be sure to use complete sentences.

A Complete each sentence with details from the box. Write the complete sentences. Then write two sentences of your own. Tell how you might have felt if you were in the science class.

simple electric circuits to learn about electricity	lightning is a form of electricity rubbing balloons on our hair

1. Today in science class I learned that _____.
2. Our teacher showed us some _____.
3. We did some experiments _____.
4. In one experiment, we created static electricity by _____.
5. _____
6. _____

B Complete each sentence with information about yourself. Then add two sentences of your own.

7. Something very special happened when I _____. 8. I will never forget the day that _____. 9. At the beginning, I _____. 10. Later, I realized that I _____. 11. _____ 12. _____

C Write a personal narrative in the form of a journal or diary. Tell what your day has been like and how you feel. Use details and complete sentences to make your personal narrative clear.

Subjects and Predicates

A **sentence** must have both a **subject** and a **predicate.** The **complete subject** is made up of all the words that tell whom or what the sentence is about. A complete subject may have several words or only one word. The most important word in the complete subject is called the **simple subject.** It is usually a noun or a pronoun. Some simple subjects, such as *North America,* have more than one word.

The **complete predicate** is made up of all the words that tell what the subject is or does. It may have several words or only one word. The most important word in the complete predicate is the verb. It is called the **simple predicate.** Some simple predicates can have more than one word, such as *will visit.*

Complete Subject   Complete Predicate

The Spanish withdrew from Mexico in 1821.

Simple Subject   Simple Predicate

The Spanish withdrew from Mexico in 1821.

 A Write each sentence. Underline the complete subject and circle the complete predicate.

1. Mexico is located to the south of the United States.
2. The United States and Mexico share a common border.
3. Both countries are major trading partners.
4. The economy of Mexico is growing fast.
5. Many goods in the United States are made in Mexico.

B Identify the underlined words in each sentence. Write **S** for subject or **P** for predicate. Then write the simple subject or the simple predicate in each of the underlined items.

1. Mexico <u>is a large country</u>.
2. <u>Mexico City</u> is the capital of Mexico.
3. The main language in Mexico <u>is Spanish</u>.
4. <u>Many Mexicans</u> also speak Indian languages.
5. Indians <u>have lived in Mexico for many years</u>.
6. <u>Latin America</u> was originally inhabited by Indians.
7. <u>The Spanish</u> settled there hundreds of years ago.
8. They <u>brought their customs and language</u>.
9. The Spanish influence <u>dominates life in Latin America</u>.
10. <u>Many newspapers</u> are written in Spanish.

C Use each pair of nouns and verbs below to write complete sentences. Underline the complete subject of each sentence. Circle the complete predicate.

11. brother   lives
12. father   works
13. uncle   plays
14. mother   will take
15. nephew   eats
16. cousins   watch
17. father-in-law   teaches
18. dog   gobbles
19. pets   play
20. cat   enjoys

Review and Assess

Read each sentence. Underline the complete subject. Circle the complete predicate.

1. I asked my friend Gina to come over for dinner.
2. My mom and dad enjoy Gina.
3. They adore her sense of humor.
4. Gina taught us some Spanish words.
5. She is a patient teacher.
6. Gina will read us a story in Spanish.
7. All of us will eat delicious tacos.
8. Mexican food can be spicy.

Read the following paragraph. Write the letter of the words that describe the underlined word or words in each sentence.

9. Jeanne <u>was the new girl at school</u>. 10. <u>Many of the students</u> teased her because she could not speak Spanish well. 11. Shy <u>Jeanne</u> wanted to fit in, but she found it difficult to learn Spanish. 12. Sometimes Jeanne <u>wished</u> she could go back to her old school. 13. She <u>will make new friends soon</u>.

9. **A** simple subject   **C** simple predicate
    B complete subject   **D** complete predicate

10. **A** simple subject   **C** simple predicate
    B complete subject   **D** complete predicate

11. **A** simple subject   **C** simple predicate
    B complete subject   **D** complete predicate

12. **A** simple subject   **C** simple predicate
    B complete subject   **D** complete predicate

13. **A** simple subject   **C** simple predicate
    B complete subject   **D** complete predicate

Adding Details to Subjects and Predicates

Add specific details to tell about the events in your personal narrative. Use these details to tell what you saw, how you felt, and what happened.

- I called my dog. She came. (few details)
- I gave a piercing whistle to my dog. Kika rushed over in a cloud of dust, with her tongue hanging out. (specific details)

A Complete the sentences below with details from the box. Write the new paragraph.

> **Saw** light blue ribbon, dirtier than an old dishrag
> **Felt** makes me happy, was quite surprised
> **What Happened** adopted a scruffy dog,
> washed her in the tub

    1. Last month my dad and I _____ from the animal shelter. **2.** She was a happy dog, but she was _____. **3.** We _____ when we first got her home. **4.** I _____ that she didn't mind being washed. **5.** My mom tied a _____ in her fur. **6.** Owning a dog _____ .

B Add details to each sentence to make this personal narrative come alive. Then write the new paragraph.

    7. I like to visit _____. (Name a place.) **8.** Going there is fun because _____. (Tell your feelings about this place.) **9.** I like to look at _____. (Tell what you see there.) **10.** The last time I was there, _____. (Tell what happened.) **11.** I want to go back again to _____. (Tell another detail about the place.)

C Write a short personal narrative about an animal you saw or played with recently. Include details to explain what happened, what you saw, and how you felt.

Four Kinds of Sentences

There are four kinds of sentences. Each begins with a capital letter and has a special end mark.

A **declarative sentence** makes a statement. It ends with a period.

> The children boarded the train.

An **interrogative sentence** asks a question. It ends with a question mark.

> Did the children board the train?

An **imperative sentence** gives a command or makes a request. It ends with a period. The subject (*you*) is not shown, but it is understood.

> Please board the train.

An **exclamatory sentence** shows strong feeling. It ends with an exclamation mark.

> What a long trip that was!

 A Write **D** if the sentence is declarative. Write **IN** if the sentence is interrogative. Write **IM** if the sentence is imperative. Write **E** if the sentence is exclamatory.

1. Do you know anybody who is adopted?
2. I was adopted as a small child.
3. How wonderful that must be!
4. Please tell me what it is like to be adopted.
5. Can you speak to my class about it?

Write each sentence. Make any necessary corrections in capitalization and punctuation.

6. are you ready to go!
7. the train is leaving soon.
8. that's great.
9. i prefer riding trains to buses?

B Complete each sentence by adding the correct end punctuation mark.

    1. Have you ever moved to a new place **2.** I moved here from Kansas when I was five **3.** What was Kansas like **4.** I don't have many memories of that time **5.** That's amazing **6.** I remember everything that has happened to me since I was born **7.** That's impossible **8.** May I ask you questions about what happened when you were young **9.** I'll be happy to tell you everything **10.** Start at the very beginning

C Complete each sentence with a word or words from the box. Write the new sentences. Then write whether the sentence is **declarative**, **interrogative**, **imperative**, or **exclamatory**.

on a school field trip last year.	is a great state!	in Illinois.
about your trip.	born in Tennessee?	
an amazing bus trip!	ever been there?	

11. Were you _____

12. No, I was born _____

13. Wow, Illinois _____

14. Have you _____

15. I went there _____

16. Tell me _____

17. It was _____

Review and Assess

Write each sentence. Add the correct capitalization and end mark.

1. i've been learning all about orphan trains
2. do you know much about them
3. these trains carried orphans who were looking for homes
4. what an interesting story this is from American history
5. would you like to learn about orphan trains
6. go to the library to learn more about them
7. the library has many great books about these trains
8. you can also research orphan trains on the Internet

Read the following paragraph. Write the letter of the word that tells about each sentence.

9. Look at that train. 10. High-speed trains can travel over one hundred miles an hour. 11. Wow, that's fast! 12. Have you ever been on a high-speed train? 13. Passengers in Europe and Japan often ride on high-speed trains.

9. **A** declarative   **C** imperative
    B interrogative   **D** exclamatory

10. **A** declarative   **C** imperative
     B interrogative   **D** exclamatory

11. **A** declarative   **C** imperative
     B interrogative   **D** exclamatory

12. **A** declarative   **C** imperative
     B interrogative   **D** exclamatory

13. **A** declarative   **C** imperative
     B interrogative   **D** exclamatory

Varying Sentences

Use different kinds of sentences to make your writing style exciting.
For instance, begin or end your narrative with an interrogative or an
exclamatory sentence.

- <u>Have you ever taken a train across the country?</u> instead of <u>I took a train trip.</u>
- <u>What a great trip it was!</u> instead of <u>I thought it was a great trip.</u>

A The first three sentences below might begin a personal narrative. Write
each of these sentences as an interrogative sentence. The next three
sentences might end a personal narrative. Rewrite each of these sentences
as an exclamatory sentence.

1. Chicago is the best place for a holiday vacation.
2. You can imagine why I'd visit Chicago in December.
3. A ten-hour train trip can be exciting.
4. Is Chicago a fascinating city?
5. Will I ever forget this wonderful vacation?
6. Were the holiday decorations amazing?

B Write your own interrogative sentence to begin this personal narrative.
Write an exclamatory sentence at the end. Add end marks to each sentence.
Write the paragraph.

　　　　7. _____　　**8.** At first I thought the train would get to Chicago
in no time at all　**9.** As the train sped along, I gazed out the window
at the beautiful scenery　**10.** However, every hour or two we stopped
at another station　**11.** I couldn't believe it　**12.** At each stop I became
more and more frustrated　**13.** Why was this trip taking so long
14. _____

C Write a short personal narrative about a trip you took. Vary your
sentences to add style to your writing.

Compound and Complex Sentences

A **simple sentence** expresses a complete thought. A **compound sentence** contains two or more simple sentences joined by a comma and a conjunction such as *and, but,* or *or.*

Simple sentence: Ken collects baseball cards.
Compound sentence: Ken collects baseball cards, and he trades them too.

A **clause** is a group of words that has a subject and a predicate. An **independent clause** can stand alone. A **dependent clause** cannot stand alone.

| Independent Clause | Dependent Clause |

Ken sorted his cards before he gave one to Larry.

A **complex sentence** contains an independent clause and one or more dependent clauses. The clauses can be connected with a word such as *if, because, before, after, since,* or *when.* Use a comma when the dependent clause begins the sentence.

Complex sentence: If a card is rare, it could be very expensive.

 Read each sentence. Write **compound** if the sentence is a compound sentence. Write **complex** if the sentence is a complex sentence.

1. Some baseball cards are valuable, and some are rare.
2. Since they can get damaged easily, hold the cards carefully.
3. Many cards are common, and you can collect them easily.
4. If you want to collect new cards, buy them from a store.
5. Mira looked calm, but she was actually quite nervous.
6. The pitch zoomed toward her, and she began to swing.
7. When the pitcher began his windup, she kept her eye on the ball.

B Write the word you would use (and, or, or but) to join these simple sentences to form compound sentences.

1. My brother is shorter than I am. He can jump higher.
2. I like to play catch with him. He likes to play catch with me too.
3. On weekends we go to the park. We stay home and do homework.
4. I like pitching. I do not have a good curve ball.
5. My brother is a fantastic hitter. He is an above-average fielder too.

C Add a clause from the box to complete each sentence. Write **compound** or **complex** to tell what kind of sentence each one is.

> If the ball was within reach
> Willie was near the end of his career
> but his manager kept him in the lineup
> Willie spent many years with the Giants
> but he was also an outstanding fielder
> and he was one of the greatest players of all time

6. Willie Mays played for the Giants, _____.
7. His career began slowly, _____.
8. He was famous for hitting home runs, _____.
9. _____, he would be sure to catch it.
10. _____ before he was traded to the Mets.
11. When he was traded to the Mets, _____.

Review and Assess

Read each sentence. Write **I** if the underlined words are an independent clause. Write **D** if the underlined words are a dependent clause.

1. <u>After I finished my homework</u>, I went to baseball practice.
2. <u>I practiced hitting</u>, and I worked on my fielding.
3. I tried hard, but <u>I still couldn't hit the ball very often</u>.
4. My coach gave me some tips, but <u>they did not seem to help me</u>.
5. <u>Since it was my first year on the team</u>, I still had a lot to learn.
6. I promised to work even harder, and <u>I was willing to be patient</u>.
7. <u>Even though the bat cracked</u>, I hit the ball out of the park.

Write the letter that tells about each underlined word or group of words.

8. Richard likes sports, <u>but</u> he prefers to read.

   A conjunction   **C** dependent clause
   B independent clause   **D** complex sentence

9. <u>He usually reads novels</u>, but he will read a biography every so often.

   A compound sentence   **C** dependent clause
   B independent clause   **D** complex sentence

10. <u>When he is bored, he often goes to the library to look for a good book</u>.

    A compound sentence   **C** dependent clause
    B independent clause   **D** complex sentence

11. <u>He often brings his sister with him, or sometimes he goes alone</u>.

    A compound sentence   **C** dependent clause
    B independent clause   **D** complex sentence

12. <u>While he reads</u>, his sister enjoys looking at picture books.

    A compound sentence   **C** dependent clause
    B independent clause   **D** complex sentence

Improving Your Sentences

Avoid short, choppy sentences by combining them into compound or complex sentences. Compound and complex sentences can make your writing more varied and interesting.

- I like baseball. I like football. I like soccer the most. (choppy)
- I like baseball and football, but I like soccer the most. (better)

A Combine each pair of choppy sentences below, using the word in ( ). Remember to add a comma. Add a closing sentence. Write the paragraph.

1. Dark clouds loomed above. I hoped it would not rain. (but) **2.** I was scheduled to pitch today. I did not want the game to be canceled. (and) **3.** Luckily, the sun poked through the clouds. We would have had to play the game next week. (or) **4.** I pitched a great game. The score was still close. (but) **5.** I struck out the final batter to end the game. My teammates cheered. (and) **6.** _____

B Complete the sentences below by making them compound or complex sentences. Write the new sentences. Then write a closing sentence. The first one is done for you.

7. <u>When I made the baseball team</u>, I jumped for joy. **8.** The competition was tough, _____. **9.** If I had not made the team, _____. **10.** I could play in the outfield, _____. **11.** I have a strong arm, _____. **12.** When I have to throw a runner out, _____. **13.** _____, I want to be a starter. **14.** _____

C Write a short personal narrative about a time you played a sport or attended a sporting event. Include compound and complex sentences to add variety to your writing.

Correcting Sentence Fragments and Run-ons

A **sentence fragment** may begin with a capital letter and end with a period, but it does not express a complete thought. Some fragments can be corrected by adding words to make a complete sentence.

Sentence fragment: Early in the morning.
Corrected sentence: My school bus comes early in the morning.

Some fragments can be corrected by attaching them to a related sentence.

Sentence and a fragment: I wait for the bus. At the corner.
Corrected sentence: I wait for the bus at the corner.

A **run-on sentence** is two or more sentences combined with just a comma, or with no conjunction or punctuation at all. Correct a run-on sentence by writing two separate sentences or by changing it to a compound sentence.

Run-on sentence: My best friend is Velma I meet her on the bus each day.
Separate sentences: My best friend is Velma. I meet her on the bus each day.
Compound sentence: My best friend is Velma, and I meet her on the bus each day.

 A Read each group of words. Write **F** if the group of words is a sentence fragment. Write **S** if it is a complete sentence.

1. I never get tired of playing with my friends in our neighborhood.
2. Where the playground is down by the school.
3. Game with three balls and a bat.
4. I couldn't believe it when I hit a home run yesterday.
5. My new house was built last year, and I moved with my family.
6. And the sunlight.
7. I sleep in the same room with my sister, and she snores loudly.

B Correct each run-on sentence. Write a compound sentence by adding a comma and the conjunction *and, but,* or *or.*

1. Some cities are huge there are many things to do.
2. Las Vegas was once small now it is quite large.
3. Los Angeles is enormous Los Alamos is not very large.
4. Life in a large city can be hectic it can be exciting.
5. Some people dislike cities they would rather live in a small town.
6. Small towns are quiet there is often less to do there.
7. Most very small towns have a few stores they have one general store.
8. A general store sells basic items you can also buy food there.
9. Some people go to cities for supplies they buy special foods too.
10. Will you live in a large city would you rather live in a small town?
11. My grandmother grew up in a city she liked it better than our small town.
12. I love to visit the city my small town will always be home.

C Correct each fragment. Write the sentences.

13. My oldest cousin, Martine.
14. Drops by in the evenings.
15. To be a doctor and find cures for diseases.
16. Studies all the time.
17. Her heavy knapsack.
18. Lugs it wherever she goes.
19. Helps me with my math homework.
20. Sometimes braids my hair.
21. A wonderful relative.
22. Be just like her.

Review and Assess

Read each group of words. Write **F** if the group of words is a sentence fragment. Write **RO** if the group of words is a run-on sentence. Write **S** if the group of words is a complete sentence.

1. I take my sister to the playground every afternoon.
2. She plays hopscotch she swings on the swing.
3. Plays in the sandbox with her friends.
4. She makes a sand castle then she makes a moat.
5. Her best friend Anita Johnson.

Each of these is a sentence fragment. Write the letter of the word or words that corrects each fragment.

6. was excited about my part in the school play.
7. My part in the play.   8. studied our lines every day.
9. On opening night.   10. Fortunately, none of us.

6. **A** Today   **C** School
   B Happy   **D** I

7. **A** or want   **C** part in the play
   B was not big   **D** acting

8. **A** My friends and I   **C** Always
   B Director   **D** Forgot

9. **A** and my classmates   **C** began to get
   B incredibly nervous   **D** we were nervous

10. **A** forgot our lines   **C** bad dreams
    B in the theater   **D** we

Editing Your Writing

Fragments and run-on sentences will confuse or distract your reader. Use complete sentences to write a personal narrative that is clear and flows well.

A Correct the fragment and the run-on sentence in this paragraph. Then write a closing sentence for the paragraph.

1. We live in Seattle, which has grown quite busy in the last few years. **2.** <u>I like to watch baseball games my sister takes me to the ballpark.</u> **3.** We saw the Mariners, who are a very good team. **4.** The Dodgers had a grand slam in the third inning. **5.** <u>A close</u> game.
6. _____

B Read each group of words below. If the group of words is a fragment, add words to make it a complete sentence. If the group of words is a run-on sentence, change it to a compound sentence, or write it as two sentences. Then write two sentences of your own to complete the paragraph.

7. People in my neighborhood. **8.** Many different kinds of people live here they are old and young. **9.** Live about a mile from my school. **10.** My brother walks with me to school, we take the bus. **11.** Sometimes I run into friends we walk together. **12.** Do homework together. **13.** Then we play in the park we race home for dinner. **14.** _____ **15.** _____

C Write a personal narrative about a typical day in your neighborhood. Make sure your sentences are constructed correctly.

Writing a Personal Narrative

A **test** may ask you to write a personal narrative. Use time-order words such as *first* and *next* to show when things happen. Write your narrative so that it flows smoothly from the beginning to the middle to the end. Follow the tips below.

> **TIMED TESTS**
>
> You might divide your time for a 45 minute test this way:
> **PLAN: 10 minutes;**
> **WRITE: 25 minutes;**
> **CHECK YOUR WORK: 10 minutes.**

Understand the prompt. Make sure you know what to do. Read the prompt carefully. A prompt for a personal narrative could look like this:

> **Think about an exciting experience or memorable event in your life. Write a personal narrative about it.**

Key words and phrases are *experience, event in your life,* and *personal narrative.*

Find a good topic. Visualize important events in your life and make a list. Choose an event that has interesting or exciting details.

Organize your ideas. Write a time line on scratch paper to help organize the order of events.

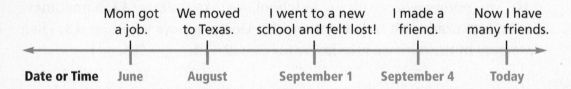

	Mom got a job.	We moved to Texas.	I went to a new school and felt lost!	I made a friend.	Now I have many friends.
Date or Time	June	August	September 1	September 4	Today

Write a good beginning. A good introductory sentence will grab your reader's attention.

Develop and elaborate ideas. Use your time line to organize events. Include vivid words and a variety of sentence types. Use complete sentences.

Write a strong ending. Consider ending your personal narrative by describing how you felt about the events that took place.

Check your work. Decide if anything needs to be changed or corrected.

See how the personal narrative below addresses the prompt, flows from the beginning to the middle to the end, and strongly expresses the writer's voice.

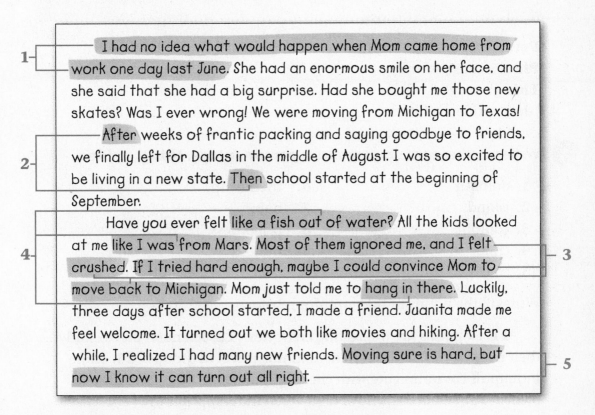

1— I had no idea what would happen when Mom came home from work one day last June. She had an enormous smile on her face, and she said that she had a big surprise. Had she bought me those new skates? Was I ever wrong! We were moving from Michigan to Texas!

2— After weeks of frantic packing and saying goodbye to friends, we finally left for Dallas in the middle of August. I was so excited to be living in a new state. Then school started at the beginning of September.

4— Have you ever felt like a fish out of water? All the kids looked at me like I was from Mars. Most of them ignored me, and I felt —3 crushed. If I tried hard enough, maybe I could convince Mom to move back to Michigan. Mom just told me to hang in there. Luckily, three days after school started, I made a friend. Juanita made me feel welcome. It turned out we both like movies and hiking. After a while, I realized I had many new friends. Moving sure is hard, but —5 now I know it can turn out all right.

1. The first sentence grabs the reader's attention.
2. The writer clearly shows the flow of events.
3. Compound and complex sentences make the writing clear.
4. Vivid words and phrases strengthen the writer's voice.
5. This strong ending shows the writer's feelings about moving.

Nouns

A **noun** is a word that names one or more persons, places, or things. Some nouns name things you cannot see, such as ideas or feelings. Nouns may be found in the subject of a sentence, in the predicate, or in both the subject and predicate.

Person: swimmer, engineer
Place: coast, island
Thing: snorkel, whale
Idea: pride, beauty

 Write whether each noun names a **person, place, thing,** or **idea.**

1. dolphin
2. island
3. captain
4. child
5. coast

6. friendship
7. baby
8. happiness
9. honesty
10. beach

Write all the nouns in the paragraph below.

    11. Dolphins are interesting creatures. **12.** Scientists like to study their behavior. **13.** Most often, dolphins travel in groups. **14.** These mammals communicate with clicking sounds, whistles, and assorted bleats. **15.** Researchers have discovered that dolphins are very intelligent animals.

B Write each sentence. Circle the nouns that are used in the subject. Underline the nouns that are used in the predicate.

1. Some people look for lost treasure on sunken boats.
2. A few explorers have found chests filled with gold.
3. Many underwater explorers look for information about the past.
4. Divers search the water for traces of ancient boats.
5. Old ships reveal valuable clues about ancient people.
6. Scientists study the pots and dishes found in wrecks.
7. The contents of the pots indicate the goods that were shipped.
8. These pots also provide information about foods long ago.
9. Historians study shipwrecks along ancient trading routes.
10. The undersea world provides a glimpse into life long ago.

C Write a noun from the box to complete each sentence. Write the paragraph.

sun	afternoon	beach
umbrella	morning	back

11. I love to go to the _____. **12.** Sometimes I just lie on my _____ and watch the clouds sweep by. **13.** I enjoy the beach the most in the _____, right after breakfast. **14.** Later on, in the _____, the sun can be very hot. **15.** I try to stay under my _____ to avoid getting too much _____.

Review and Assess

Write the sentences. Underline all the nouns in each sentence.

1. The turtle swims to shore and lays eggs.
2. Three playful dolphins frolic in the surf.
3. Whales swim through the waves with a gigantic splash.
4. A fierce shark darts through the ocean.
5. Under the water, the lobsters flex powerful claws.
6. Birds bob and float on the calm water.
7. Suddenly, the wind blows strongly.
8. The birds fly quickly to the safe, quiet island.

Read each sentence. Write the letter of the word that is a noun.

9. The sea is calm and the waves are gentle.

   A calm **C** waves

   B are **D** gentle

10. A young girl fishes off the side of the dock.

    A young **C** fishes

    B girl **D** off

11. No fish are biting, and the girl decides to give up.

    A fish **C** decides

    B are **D** up

12. She stays by the dock and admires the beauty of the colorful sunset.

    A stays **C** admires

    B beauty **D** colorful

13. As the sun slips past the horizon, she walks home slowly.

    A slips **C** sun

    B past **D** slowly

Using Exact Nouns in Descriptions

Use exact nouns to add power to your writing. Look at the nouns in the first sentence below. See how exact nouns make the new sentence clearer and more vivid.

- The <u>animal</u> dangled its <u>legs</u>.
- The <u>octopus</u> dangled its <u>tentacles</u>.

A Improve the paragraph below by replacing the underlined words with words from the box. Write the word you choose for each sentence.

tanks	cafeteria	weekend
sandwiches	whales	gallons

1. Every week I visit the <u>animals</u> in the aquarium. **2.** The whales' <u>places</u> are enormous. **3.** I bet they hold over a million <u>things</u> of water. **4.** Next <u>time</u> I am going to the aquarium with my mother. **5.** She promises she will bring plenty of <u>food</u> so that we can have a picnic. **6.** We like to eat outside, next to the <u>building</u>.

B Replace the underlined word with a more exact noun of your own. Write the words you choose.

7. I live right down the block from the <u>water</u>. **8.** I love the sound of waves crashing on the <u>ground</u>. **9.** There is something soothing about listening to the <u>sound</u> of the waves. **10.** Often, I go to the <u>place</u> to watch when a boat is approaching.

C Write a short description about your favorite place. Use exact nouns to make your description clear and exciting.

Proper Nouns

A **proper noun** names a particular person, place, or thing. Begin the first word and every other important word in a proper noun with a capital letter. Nouns that are not proper nouns are called **common nouns.** Common nouns are not capitalized.

Common nouns: teacher, school, country

Proper nouns: Natania Wright, Wilmington School, United States of America

 A Write **CN** if the underlined item in each sentence is a common noun. Write **PN** if the underlined item in each sentence is a proper noun.

1. Many <u>storms</u> have damaged the east coast of our country.
2. <u>Florida</u> is often pummeled by tremendous storms.
3. One of the worst storms ever, <u>Hurricane Andrew</u>, struck in 1992.
4. Scientists at the <u>National Hurricane Center</u> predict storms.
5. The <u>center</u> is located in Miami.
6. Many <u>scientists</u> track storms during hurricane season.

Write the sentences. Underline the proper nouns in each sentence.

7. Florida is one of fifty states in the United States.
8. Rhode Island is the smallest state.
9. Alaska is the largest state, followed by Texas and then California.
10. Have you ever been to another continent, such as Africa or Asia?
11. Rhonda Forrest, my next-door neighbor, comes from Great Britain.
12. Rhonda became a citizen of the United States last July.
13. She was sworn in as a citizen at City Hall.
14. The judge, Karen Smith, congratulated Rhonda.
15. Dawn Forrest hugged her mother proudly.

B Capitalize each proper noun. Write each incorrect common noun with a small letter. Write the new sentences.

1. marvin keynes went on a Trip to europe.
2. Marvin left at the beginning of july and returned in late august.
3. Marvin traveled in italy and switzerland.
4. He spent the Month of july in rome.
5. Rome, the capital of italy, is a fascinating Place.
6. He also visited an ancient Temple, called the pantheon.
7. Marvin slept during the Flight back to new york.
8. Mr. and Mrs. keynes met him at john f. kennedy international airport.
9. When marvin arrived home, his Dog fluffy jumped all over him!
10. uncle charlie had been taking care of the dog.
11. Next Summer Marvin will drive to yellowstone park and take the dog along.

C Write a proper noun of your own for each common noun. Then write three sentences using some of the proper nouns.

12. city
13. river
14. park
15. school
16. building
17. mountain
18. person
19. day
20. teacher
21. country

Review and Assess

Write **CN** if the underlined item in each sentence is a common noun.
Write **PN** if the underlined item in each sentence is a proper noun.

1. <u>Mr. Grisman</u> became a pilot for Speedy Airlines in 1995.
2. He flies passengers to <u>destinations</u> all over the world.
3. Last <u>Friday</u> he flew to Kenya.
4. On the trip back, he experienced turbulent <u>weather</u>.
5. Mr. Grisman lives in Silver Spring, <u>Maryland</u>.

Read each sentence. Write the letter of the word
or group of words that is a proper noun.

6. Several million people live in Los Angeles, California.

    A Several   **C** people
    B million   **D** California

7. Some of the people in Los Angeles come from countries such as Russia.

    A Some   **C** Russia
    B people   **D** countries

8. Every year, people come to Los Angeles to try to become movie stars.

    A year   **C** Los Angeles
    B people   **D** movie stars

9. This sprawling city is the capital of the movie industry in the United States.

    A city   **C** movie industry
    B capital   **D** United States

10. Hollywood has many movie studios and film crews.

    A Hollywood   **C** movie studios
    B many   **D** film crews

Using Proper Nouns in Descriptions

Proper nouns in your descriptions give your readers an exact picture. See how proper nouns in the second sentence below make information more specific.

- <u>The storm</u> weakened when it passed over <u>the island</u>.
- <u>Hurricane Andrew</u> weakened when it passed over <u>Puerto Rico</u>.

A Replace the underlined word or words with a proper noun from the box. Then add a closing sentence with a proper noun. Write the paragraph.

Indiana	Lincoln Elementary School	
Pass Avenue	February	Mrs. Holmes

1. Last <u>month</u> there was a tremendous snowstorm. **2.** Most of <u>the state</u> was shut down. **3.** Even <u>my school</u> was closed. **4.** I helped <u>my neighbor</u> shovel the snow out of her driveway. **5.** The snowdrifts were piled high on <u>a street</u>. **6.** _____

B Replace the underlined words with proper nouns of your own. Add a closing sentence with a proper noun. Write the paragraph.

7. I live in <u>a town</u>, which I think is a wonderful place. **8.** Every weekday I attend <u>school</u>. **9.** Sometimes my family and I go to <u>a restaurant</u> and have a delicious meal. **10.** This restaurant is on <u>a street</u>. **11.** One of the best places in town is <u>the movie theater</u>, especially on a rainy day. **12.** Even people from <u>the next town</u> go there to laugh and have a good time. **13.** _____

C Write a short description about a big storm or other weather event that you remember. Include proper nouns to give your readers an exact picture.

Plural Nouns

Plural nouns name more than one person, place, or thing. Look at the rules below to see how plural nouns are formed.

- Add -**s** to most singular nouns to form the plural.

    meal/meals   job/jobs   baker/bakers   hand/hands

- Add -**es** to singular nouns ending in **ch, sh**, **x, z, s**, and **ss.**

    lunch/lunches   wish/wishes   fox/foxes   bus/buses   class/classes

- If a noun ends in a **vowel** and **y,** add -**s.**

    monkey/monkeys   ray/rays   Monday/Mondays

- If a noun ends in a **consonant** and **y,** change **y** to **i** and add -**es.**

    pony/ponies   lady/ladies   blueberry/blueberries   city/cities

- Some nouns have **irregular plural** forms. You will need to memorize the spelling changes for nouns such as these. Use a dictionary to help you.

    man/men   goose/geese   foot/feet   child/children

- For many nouns ending in **f** or **fe,** change **f** or **fe** to **v** and add -**es.**

    self/selves   loaf/loaves   leaf/leaves   knife/knives   scarf/scarves

- Some nouns have the same singular and plural forms.

    deer   sheep   moose   series   headquarters   fish

A Write the sentences. Underline the plural nouns in each sentence.

1. My brother grows flowers in the garden.
2. Last year, he grew daisies, marigolds, and petunias.
3. Last week, he built a fence to keep out the deer and the rabbits.
4. He usually works in the garden during evenings and weekends.
5. Men and women from the neighborhood keep him company while he works.

B Write the plural form of each noun. Use a dictionary if you need help.

1. park *parks*
2. sandwich *sandwiches*
3. woman *women*
4. home *home*
5. loaf *loaves*
6. city *cities*
7. sky *skies*
8. charity *charities*
9. goose *geese*
10. boss *bosses*
11. watch *watches*

12. man *men*
13. foot *feet*
14. lady *ladies*
15. ax *axes*
16. child *children*
17. mattress *mattresses*
18. supply *supplies*
19. life *lifes*
20. tooth *teeth*
21. mouse *mouses*
22. family *families*

C Complete each sentence with a plural noun. Write the sentences.

23. Many _____ need volunteers.
24. Have you or your _____ ever volunteered?
25. Some volunteers work in _____ or in hospitals.
26. Volunteers help make our _____ strong.
27. If you wish to help a charity, just put your donations in _____.
28. You can donate old _____ or toys.
29. Ask your _____ to help you clean up an abandoned lot.

Review and Assess

Change each underlined singular noun to its plural form.

volunteers
1. <u>Volunteer</u> are needed in every community.
children
2. Nancy tutors <u>child</u> in her class.
magazines
3. Samuel donates old books and <u>magazine</u> to his library.
citizens
4. Roberta's class volunteers on weekends to help senior <u>citizen</u>.
toddlers
5. During the summer, Alphonso teaches <u>toddler</u> to swim.
supplies
6. Animal shelters are always in need of <u>supply</u>.
students
7. Will you join these <u>student</u> and help others in need?
charities
8. All the <u>charity</u> will really appreciate your help.

Write the letter of the word that correctly completes each sentence.

9. Many _____ donate day-old bread to charity.

   A bakery   C bakerys
   (B) bakeries   D bakeryes

10. The day-old _____ of bread are still tasty and nutritious.

    A loafes   C loafs
    B loavs   **(D)** loaves

11. Men and _____ volunteer to help deliver the bread to shelters.

    A womens   **(C)** women
    B woman   D women's

12. They carry the bread in cardboard _____.

    (A) boxes   C box
    B boxs   D boxess

13. Where would our _____ be without volunteers?

    A communitys   **(C)** communities
    B communites   D community's

Using Plural Nouns in Descriptions

Add interesting details to your sentences to create a vivid word picture.
Spell plural nouns correctly.

- **No:** Many charitys help improve the lives of childs.
- **Yes:** Many caring charities help improve the lives of needy children.

A Write the plural form of each noun in ( ). Add a word from the box that describes each noun and makes sense. Write the sentences.

clattering	spicy	ripe	steamy	thick

1. At the Community Kitchen, volunteers serve big, _____ (sandwich) to hungry people. **2.** I work as a volunteer, putting red, _____ (berry) on ice cream for dessert. **3.** The adult volunteers dish out hot, _____ (pot) of soup. **4.** Sometimes we serve _____ (sauce) over beans and rice. **5.** I love this noisy kitchen with its sounds of _____ (knife) and forks.

B Write the correct plural of each noun in ( ). Add a word of your own to describe each plural noun. Write the paragraph.

6. Have you ever cleaned up _____ (table) or done any other volunteer work in your town? **7.** Maybe you have served _____ (lunch) to a group of people. **8.** In some places during autumn, young people rake _____ (leaf) for neighbors. **9.** Helping _____ (family) can make you feel like a supporter of the community. **10.** Some day any of us might need help to overcome our own _____ (trouble).

C Write a brochure for an organization or a group that helps people in your community. Use interesting details that paint a clear picture of the organization and what it does.

Possessive Nouns

A **possessive noun** shows ownership. A **singular possessive noun** shows that one person, place, or thing has or owns something. A **plural possessive noun** shows that more than one person, place, or thing has or owns something.

- To make a singular noun show possession, add an **apostrophe (')** and **-s**.

    the questions of the child   the child**'s** questions

- When a plural noun ends in **-s**, add an **apostrophe (')** to make the noun show possession.

    the nests of the birds   the birds' nests

- When a plural noun does not end in **-s**, add an **apostrophe (')** and **-s** to show possession.

    the stories of the men   the men**'s** stories

 A Write the correct possessive noun to complete each sentence.

1. (Florida's, Floridas') Everglades are endangered. **2.** This (park's, parks's) environment became threatened because of too much development around it. **3.** Many (people's, peoples') efforts are helping to restore the swamp's water resources. **4.** Everglades National Park was established in 1947 to protect the (area's, areas') natural condition. **5.** New laws saved many (animals', animal's) habitats.

Write each noun below as a possessive noun. Write **S** if the possessive noun is singular. Write **P** if the possessive noun is plural.

6. alligator   **10.** child

7. women   **11.** story

8. islands   **12.** birds

9. Indian   **13.** countries

B Add an apostrophe (') or an apostrophe (') and **-s** to make each underlined word possessive.

1. I climbed in the rowboat by the <u>lake</u> edge.
2. One <u>camera</u> bag was stashed in a waterproof container.
3. Several <u>alligators</u> heads appeared by the shore.
4. I paddled away to avoid those <u>creatures</u> menacing stares.
5. The <u>sun</u> rays reflected the still water.
6. My <u>rowboat</u> wake left a ripple in the water.
7. The flapping of several <u>hawks</u> wings interrupted the silence.
8. They were so close that I saw their <u>wings</u> feathers.
9. I took a photograph with my oldest <u>brother</u> camera.
10. Jim also likes to photograph <u>nature</u> wonders.
11. <u>Jim</u> pictures have won several awards.

C Change each underlined phrase to show possession. Write the sentences.

12. Many of the <u>habitats of the Earth</u> need to be protected.
13. The <u>fish of the oceans</u> are threatened by pollution.
14. Scientists study <u>effects of pollution</u> on wildlife.
15. The <u>findings of scientists</u> show that we need to protect wildlife.
16. What can we do to protect the <u>environment of the world</u>?
17. Some say that <u>the use by people</u> of cars should be monitored.
18. <u>Suggestions of citizens</u> include establishing wildlife refuges.
19. We need to work hard to save the <u>resources of the planet</u>.

Review and Assess

Write each word as a possessive noun.

1. car
2. mice
3. card
4. owl
5. babies
6. Chris
7. libraries
8. Earth
9. neighbor
10. animals
11. wolf
12. Mr. Hill
13. Lily
14. streets
15. alligators
16. men

Write the letter of the word that correctly completes each sentence.

17. That _____ source is unknown.

    A rivers
    B river's
    C rivers'
    D rivers's

18. A few of our _____ rivers remain unexplored.

    A countrys'
    B country's
    C countrie's
    D countries's

19. Many of the _____ resources are limited.

    A worlds
    B worlds's
    C worlds'
    D world's

20. Other _____ leaves can be used to make medicine.

    A plant's
    B plants'
    C plants
    D plants's

21. Our _____ future depends on saving the environment.

    A childs'
    B children
    C children's
    D childrens'

Using Possessive Nouns in Descriptions

Possessive nouns can make your descriptions less wordy. See how adding a possessive noun can make sentences flow more smoothly.

- The <u>voice of the storyteller</u> was deep.
- The <u>storyteller's voice</u> was deep.

A Make each sentence less wordy by replacing the underlined words with a possessive noun phrase. Write the sentences.

1. <u>The son of my neighbor</u> planted a garden in an abandoned lot. **2.** He borrowed <u>the trucks of his friends</u> to haul away the trash. **3.** Many of <u>the friends of my brother</u> helped too. **4.** They planted flowers and vegetables in the <u>soil of the garden</u>. **5.** Now everybody enjoys the <u>garden of the neighborhood</u>.

B Add your own possessive noun to complete each sentence. Write each sentence.

6. We love listening to my _____ stories about nature. **7.** _____ favorite stories are about animals. **8.** I like it when all the _____ sounds are like human voices. **9.** One interesting story tells about a young girl who finds a _____ nest. **10.** The startled _____ instincts are to protect her young. **11.** She flees with them into the _____ safe cover.

C Write a short description about your favorite place in nature. Try to use possessive nouns to make your writing smooth and less wordy.

Commas in Series and in Direct Address

A **comma** tells a reader when to pause. A list of three or more nouns forms a **series.** Use a comma after each word in a series except the last.

My dad brought home muffins, bread, and crackers from the bakery.

When you speak or write to someone, you often use that person's name or title. This use of a noun is called **direct address.** One comma sets off the noun when it appears at the beginning or the end of a sentence. Two commas are used when it appears in the middle.

Sarah, may I have a piece of bread?

What kind of bread do you want, Mark?

That slice of rye, Sarah, would be fine!

 A Add commas to each sentence to set off nouns used in a series or in direct address. Write the sentences.

1. Renata who is your favorite mystery writer?
2. That is a good question Gwen.
3. I like Raymond Chandler Agatha Christie and Arthur Conan Doyle.
4. What a wonderful list Gwen!
5. I like to read mysteries when I ride on a train bus or plane.
6. Tell me Renata what do you like to read?
7. My shelves are bursting with mysteries novels and history books.
8. Histories biographies and short stories are my favorites Gwen.
9. I guess we both like to read Renata don't we?
10. Will you lend me some books Renata?
11. Do you want to read fiction nonfiction or a biography first?
12. I'll start with nonfiction Renata.

B Complete the sentences by adding the nouns below each sentence. Remember to use commas to separate words in a series. Write the sentences.

1. Jewelers sell _____ _____ and _____.
   diamonds   emeralds   pearls

2. _____ _____ and _____ solved many mysteries.
   Sherlock Holmes   Philip Marlowe   Goldy Bear

3. Private detectives use _____ _____ and _____ to solve crimes.
   clues   disguises   deduction

4. In stakeouts, detectives use _____ _____ and _____.
   binoculars   microphones   video cameras

5. Mr. Holmes, I believe you are the best _____ _____ and _____ ever!
   detective   problem-solver   thinker

6. Do you prefer to read _____ _____ or _____?
   novels   mysteries   short stories

C Write a sentence to answer each question.

7. What are your three favorite movies?
8. What are your three favorite books?
9. What are your three favorite games?
10. What are your three favorite colors?
11. What are your three favorite foods?
12. What are your three favorite sports?
13. What are your three favorite summer activities?
14. What are your three favorite winter activities?
15. What are your three favorite animals?

Review and Assess

Add commas where they are needed. Write the sentences.

1. I like to take pictures of animals people and buildings.
2. Here is a picture I took of Mary Gina and their teacher.
3. That's a great photograph Larry!
4. Thanks Jerry I'm happy you like it.
5. Jerry hand me that camera.
6. Let me take a picture of you your dog and your brother.
7. Stand by the tree Jerry and we can get started.
8. Can I get a copy of the picture Larry after you develop it?

Write the letter of the word or words and punctuation that complete each sentence correctly.

9. Detectives look for clues such as _____ footprints, and hairs.

   A fingerprints   C fingerprints,
   B fingerprints;   D fingerprints.

10. Mr. Jones searched the house, _____ and the driveway.

   A the, yard   C the yard.
   B the yard,   D the, yard,

11. What do you think about _____ Jones?

   A this, Sergeant   C this Sergeant
   B this and Sergeant,   D this, Sergeant,

12. I think a fox, an owl, and a _____ together.

   A rabbit, worked   C rabbit worked
   B rabbit worked,   D rabbit worked.

13. You solved the _____ Jones!

   A mystery Sergeant   C mystery, Sergeant.
   B mystery Sergeant,   D mystery, Sergeant

Using Commas for Clear Writing

Use commas to make your sentences clear.

- **Unclear:** Look here Eric! I found the ball bag and glove that you lost.
- **Clear:** Look here, Eric! I found the ball, bag, and glove that you lost.

A Make the paragraph clear by adding commas to complete each sentence. Add a closing sentence of your own. Write the paragraph.

1. Ken I was so upset when I lost my grandfather's watch. **2.** I have lost things such as pencils books and magazines. **3.** Ken I had never lost anything so valuable. **4.** I looked for it here there and everywhere. **5.** Then I thoroughly searched through dozens of drawers shelves and boxes. **6.** Can you imagine Ken how happy I was when I found it? **7.** _____

B Complete each sentence with your own words. Add commas so that each sentence is clear. Write the sentences.

8. Have you ever lost something _____? (name of friend)
9. I once lost my _____ and looked on the _____ _____ and _____.
10. I asked _____ _____ and _____ if they had seen it.
11. Then I asked _____ _____ and _____ to help me look for it.
12. We searched through _____ _____ and _____.
13. You should have seen us _____. (name of friend)
14. We were covered with _____ _____ and _____.
15. I finally found it in my closet under _____ _____ and _____!

C Write a letter to a friend that describes something you lost and how you found it. List all the places you looked and all the people you questioned. Remember to use commas correctly.

Writing a Description

A **test** may ask you to write a description. Make sure your description uses vivid sense words and images. Follow the tips below.

APPEAL TO SENSES

Use vivid sense words to describe the sight, sound, feel, smell, and taste of things.

Understand the prompt. Make sure you know what to do. Read the prompt carefully. A prompt for a description could look like this:

> **Write a description of a place or a living thing in nature. Help readers use their senses to picture this place or thing.**

Key words and phrases are *description, senses, picture,* and *place or thing.*

Find a good topic. Think about different subjects that you could describe vividly. Make sure there are enough details about your subject to make your description exciting.

Organize your ideas. Make a description web on scratch paper. Write the name of your topic in the center circle. Write details about your topic in connected circles.

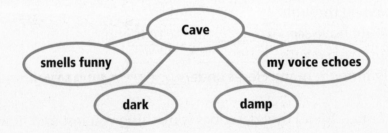

Write a good beginning. Write a catchy first sentence that makes your reader want to keep reading.

Develop and elaborate ideas. Use the subject and details from the description web to help you. Use vivid words that appeal to your reader's senses.

Write a strong ending. Consider ending your description by telling how you felt about this place or thing.

Check your work. Make any necessary changes.

See how the description below addresses the prompt, has a strong beginning and end, and uses vivid sense details.

1 — Are you afraid of the dark? If you are, you probably would hate to go to the cave in the park up the hill. But I like going there.

Even on the brightest, sunniest day, the cave is dark and gloomy. A little light gets in, so you don't really need a flashlight if you go during the daytime. The cave is not huge. It is about the size of a normal two-story house.

3 — When you walk in, you are struck by a funny smell. It smells a bit like musty clothes or books. The cave is also fairly damp, and it is always cool inside no matter how hot it is outside. In fact, I like to go there on hot days when I want to escape the terrible heat.

4 — The best thing about the cave is what happens when you yell. Your voice echoes and bounces back and forth! This cave makes me feel happy each time I go. I think anybody who is interested in nature will enjoy this extremely interesting place. — 5

1. The first sentence pulls the reader in.
2. Details show strong images and appeal to the senses.
3. Specific nouns and vivid adjectives give clear pictures.
4. The description builds to the most important quality.
5. This strong ending ties up the description.

Verbs

A complete sentence is made up of a subject and a predicate. The main word in the predicate is a **verb. Action verbs** tell what the subject of a sentence does.

Hilary <u>skipped</u> across the field.

An action verb can tell about an action that you cannot see, such as an action in someone's mind.

She <u>forgot</u> her bag.

A **linking verb** does not show action. Instead, it links, or joins, the subject to a word or words in the predicate. Linking verbs tell what the subject is or is like. Common linking verbs are forms of the verb **be,** such as *am, is, are, was,* and *were.* Other linking verbs include *become, seem, appear, feel,* and *look.*

Some kids <u>are</u> silly. They <u>seem</u> happy. She <u>is</u> the champ.

Sometimes a **helping verb** comes before the main verb. Some common helping verbs are *has, have, had, was, were, do, does, did, could, will, would,* and *should.*

I <u>am</u> <u>learning</u> to play basketball. I <u>have</u> <u>made</u> progress this year.

 Write each sentence. Circle the action verbs. Underline the linking verbs.

1. Are you a basketball fan?
2. A Canadian invented basketball.
3. Tall players enjoy a natural advantage.
4. Still, many shorter players excel.
5. Basketball is not easy.
6. Even excellent players practice.
7. Some players are better at offense.
8. Other players specialize in defense.
9. To them, defense is the key to success.

B Find the verb in each sentence. Write the action verbs in one column. Write the linking verbs in a second column. Circle helping verbs that are with a main verb.

1. The best coaches direct their players firmly.
2. Teammates should work together a few times a week.
3. Practice sessions build strong skills.
4. These sessions are important for every player.
5. Each player feels part of the team.
6. So many people have joined for a common goal.
7. Successful games are not the only goal.
8. The bonds between players and coach strengthen the whole team.

C Add a verb of your own to complete each sentence. Then write what kind of verb each one is.

9. Jenny _____ to the end of the court.
10. She _____ out of breath and weak.
11. Her coach _____ her out of the game for some rest.
12. In a few minutes, Jenny _____ much better.
13. At that moment, her team _____ by one point.
14. Jenny _____ the ball with ten seconds left.
15. She _____ to her right with the ball in her hand.
16. Her shot _____ straight and true, right through the basket.
17. The buzzer _____ and the game was over.
18. Jenny's team _____ the championship!
19. She _____ the hero of the game.
20. All her teammates _____ her for her part in their victory.

Review and Assess

Write each sentence. Circle the verb if it is an action verb.
Underline the verb if it is a linking verb.

1. Charlene works as a writer.
2. She publishes stories in magazines and on the Internet.
3. Some of her stories are fictional.
4. Editors review her stories and articles.
5. Charlene and the editors polish the stories together.

Write the letter of the words that tell about the underlined word.

6. That architect <u>is</u> building homes for a new community.

       A action verb   **C** helping verb
       B linking verb   **D** not a verb

7. They <u>create</u> blueprints that are used as plans.

       A action verb   **C** helping verb
       B linking verb   **D** not a verb

8. Architects <u>are</u> careful as they work.

       A action verb   **C** helping verb
       B linking verb   **D** not a verb

9. Some architects <u>design</u> towering skyscrapers.

       A action verb   **C** helping verb
       B linking verb   **D** not a verb

10. Others plan homes for <u>families</u>.

        A action verb   **C** helping verb
        B linking verb   **D** not a verb

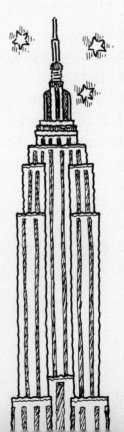

Writing with Vivid Verbs

Vivid verbs can make a comparison/contrast essay lively. Sometimes you can make your writing stronger by replacing linking verbs with action verbs. See how the vivid verb adds life and impact to the second sentence below.

- **Linking verb:** Billy <u>is</u> good at batting practice.
- **Action verb:** Billy <u>excels</u> at batting practice.

A Replace each underlined word or phrase with an action verb from the box that makes sense. Write the paragraph.

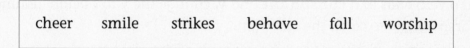

cheer	smile	strikes	behave	fall	worship

   1. I like to think I <u>am</u> like a good baseball fan. **2.** Some baseball fans <u>are devoted to</u> their teams. **3.** Other fans just <u>look happy</u> when they see a good game. **4.** I <u>am</u> somewhere in between these two types of fans. **5.** When a player on the other team <u>is</u> out, I never clap. **6.** But I still <u>am loud</u> when my team wins.

B Replace each underlined item with a vivid action verb of your own.

   7. The ball <u>is high</u> above the crowd.
   8. That shortstop <u>is fast</u> around the bases.
   9. Everyone <u>is warm</u> in the hot sun.
   10. Fans <u>are loud</u> when the home team wins.

C Write a paragraph that compares and contrasts two sports. Be sure to include vivid verbs to add interest to your writing.

Subject-Verb Agreement

The subject and the verb in a sentence must **agree** in number. A **singular subject** needs a verb that agrees with singular nouns. A **plural subject** needs a verb that agrees with plural nouns.

Use the following rules for verbs that tell about the present time.

- If the subject is a singular noun or *he, she,* or *it,* add **-s** or **-es** to most verbs: The train station <u>closes</u> at midnight. It <u>pulls</u> into the station late.

- If a verb ends in a **consonant** and **y,** change the **y** to **i** before adding **-es:** Greg <u>hurries</u> to catch the last train.

- When *you* or the singular pronoun *I* is the subject, write the verb without an **-s** or **-es:** I <u>catch</u> the early train.

- If the subject is a plural noun or a plural pronoun, do not add **-s** or **-es** to the verb: Most trains <u>arrive</u> on schedule. We seldom <u>wait</u> long.

- When nouns combine to form a compound subject with *and,* use a plural verb form: Lee and Dan <u>run</u> to the station. Planes and trains <u>are</u> good ways to travel.

- For the verb **be,** use *am* or *is* to agree with singular subjects and *are* to agree with plural subjects: I *am* on time. We *are* late.

A Write the correct form of the verb in ( ) to complete each sentence.

  1. Geraldine _____ on the platform for the train. (wait, waits)
  2. The conductors _____, "All aboard!" (yell, yells)
  3. Her parents _____ as she boards the train. (wave, waves)
  4. Geraldine _____ next to another young girl. (sit, sits)
  5. Another passenger _____ the train schedule. (study, studies)

B Add a verb to complete each sentence. Be sure to use the correct verb form. Write the sentences.

1. California _____ a big state. **2.** Many people _____ there. **3.** San Francisco and Los Angeles _____ the two biggest cities in California. **4.** In San Francisco, tourists like to _____ the trolley cars. **5.** In Los Angeles, tourists often _____ theme parks. **6.** They also like to _____ at the beach. **7.** Both residents and tourists _____ the great weather in Los Angeles. **8.** The sun _____ nearly all year. **9.** In San Francisco, however, the day often _____ with a dense fog. **10.** Sometimes the fog _____ from dawn to dusk.

C Look at the idea web below. Use the words in the idea web to write five sentences about a storm. Be sure the subjects and verbs agree.

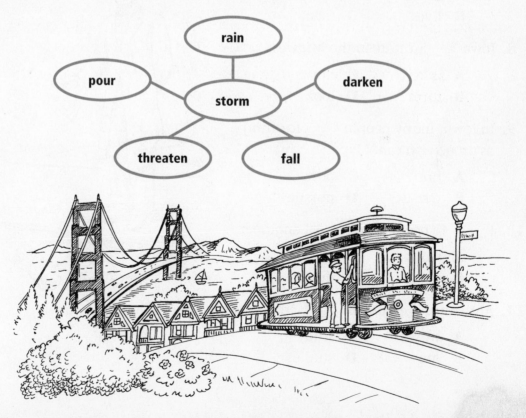

Review and Assess

Choose the correct form of the verb in ( ) to complete each sentence. Write the verbs.

1. Do you (know, knows) much about the Civil War in our country?
2. My parents and I (live, lives) near Gettysburg, Pennsylvania.
3. Gettysburg (is, are) where Abraham Lincoln made a famous speech.
4. I (believe, believes) that he wrote the speech during a train ride.
5. My teacher (explain, explains) why the Civil War was so important.
6. Some people (enjoy, enjoys) acting out Civil War battles.

Write the letter of the word that correctly completes each sentence.

7. My cousin _____ in Iowa.

    A live   **C** be
    B lives   **D** seem

8. Iowa _____ a state in the Midwest.

    A is   **C** are
    B farm   **D** look

9. In Iowa, many people _____ farming as an occupation.

    A are   **C** does
    B pursues   **D** pursue

10. I _____ to be an agricultural engineer.

    A want   **C** is
    B wants   **D** dreams

11. Agricultural engineers _____ crop rotation.

    A works   **C** study
    B are   **D** studies

Using Verbs in Comparisons

You can use vivid verbs to make comparisons. A **simile** is a comparison between two unlike things using the words *like* or *as*. A **metaphor** also makes a comparison, but it does not use *like* or *as*. Use vivid verbs with similes and metaphors to make your writing come alive.

- **Simile:** She raced <u>like</u> the wind. She dashed <u>as</u> fast as the wind.
- **Metaphor:** Her hair curled in a golden halo.

A Complete each sentence with the more vivid word in ( ). Write the word you choose. Then write **S** if the comparison is a simile, or write **M** if it is a metaphor.

1. The train (hurtled, went) along with a hurricane's power. **2.** Min (moved, wiggled) in her seat like a worm. **3.** Giant balls of smoke (billowed, went) from the train. **4.** The train (crept, went) into the station like a snail. **5.** The young girl (got, hopped) out of her seat like an excited kangaroo. **6.** She (took, dragged) her bag, which was as heavy as an anchor.

B Complete each sentence with a vivid verb of your own to form a metaphor or a simile. Write the sentences.

7. The engine _____ like a lion.

8. Sparks _____ through the air like fireworks.

9. Heavy smoke, as black as night, _____ the sky.

10. The conductor's voice was a bear's growl as he _____ "All aboard!"

11. People _____ down the platform like track stars.

12. Yellow taxis _____ a sunny circle around the station.

C Write a paragraph that compares and contrasts a train to another form of transportation. Use vivid verbs, similes, or metaphors to add excitement to your paragraph. Make sure each subject agrees with its verb.

Verb Tenses: Present, Past, and Future

The **tense** of a verb shows *when* something happens. A verb in the **present tense** shows action that happens now. A verb in the **past tense** shows action that has already happened. A verb in the **future tense** shows action that will happen.

Present-tense verbs that agree with a singular subject usually end in **-s** or **-es.**

> Willie <u>shoots</u> the marble.   He <u>flexes</u> his thumb.

Present-tense verbs that agree with plural subjects usually do not end in **-s** or **-es.**

> The players <u>shoot</u> the marbles.   They <u>flex</u> their thumbs.

Add **-ed** to most verbs to show the **past tense:** She <u>cheered</u> for her favorite team.

The spelling of some regular verbs changes when you add **-ed.**

- For verbs ending in **e,** drop the **e** and add **-ed:** loved, noted.
- For verbs ending in a **consonant** and **y,** change the **y** to **i** and add **-ed:** cried, hurried.
- For most one-syllable verbs that end in one vowel followed by one consonant, double the consonant and add **-ed:** chatted, spotted.
- Verbs that do not add **-ed** in the past tense are called **irregular verbs.** Irregular verbs do not follow a regular pattern: sat, saw, left, caught.

Verbs in the **future tense** include the helping verb *will:* We <u>will play</u> a game.

 A Write **Present, Past,** or **Future** to tell the tense of each underlined verb.

1. Louise <u>cheers</u> for her school's hockey team.
2. She <u>admires</u> the players' teamwork.
3. They almost <u>earned</u> the championship last year.
4. They <u>seem</u> even more determined now.
5. They <u>will play</u> for the championship in the spring.

B Write the correct tense for each verb below to complete each sentence. Make sure the verb agrees with the subject.

Verb	Present	Past	Future
1. like	He _____ to sing.	We _____ to sing.	They _____ to sing.
2. stay	She _____ home.	He _____ home.	I _____ home.
3. cough	He _____ loudly.	They _____ loudly.	He _____ loudly.
4. stop	It _____ working.	We _____ working.	I _____ working.
5. walk	He _____ to school.	We _____ to school.	Al _____ to school.
6. wait	Jon _____ for me.	He _____ for me.	Dad _____ for me.
7. kick	We _____ the ball.	I _____ the ball.	You _____ the ball.
8. talk	He _____ to her.	She _____ to her.	They _____ to her.
9. live	She _____ there.	I _____ there.	Marie _____ there.
10. name	He _____ the dog.	He _____ the dog.	You _____ the dog.

C Rewrite each underlined verb twice. First, change the underlined verb to the past tense. Then change the underlined verb to the future tense.

11. Rado <u>twists</u> his knee.

12. He <u>wraps</u> ice around it.

13. Then he <u>stretches</u> on the sidelines.

14. Rado <u>tries</u> to bike home.

15. Rado <u>looks</u> forward to playing again soon.

16. The team <u>needs</u> his strong kick!

17. We <u>play</u> every week.

18. Our team <u>competes</u> in the state tournament.

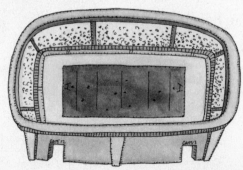

Review and Assess

Write the correct tense of the underlined verb. The word in ( ) will tell which tense to use.

1. Some athletes frequently <u>travel</u> to other countries. (past)
2. Today's athletes <u>train</u> hard, even in the off-season. (future)
3. They <u>will realize</u> that training is the key to success. (present)
4. Teamwork <u>will help</u> athletes to succeed. (present)
5. Some dedicated athletes <u>compete</u> in the Olympics. (future)

Write the letter of the verb that correctly completes each sentence.

6. Last night, I _____ catch with my brother.

   A plays   **C** play
   B will play   **D** played

7. Currently, my brother _____ college in Nebraska.

   A attend   **C** will attend
   B attends   **D** attended

8. He _____ next year.

   A graduate   **C** will graduate
   B graduated   **D** will graduated

9. Right now, he _____ to become a teacher.

   A intend   **C** will intend
   B intends   **D** intended

10. Earlier, he _____ to be a baseball umpire.

   A planned   **C** will plan
   B plan   **D** plans

Writing with Correct Verb Tenses

When you write, choose your words carefully. Use lively verbs in the correct tense to show when events occur.

- At first, I <u>played</u> marbles like a beginner. Then I <u>learned</u> some tricks and techniques. Now I <u>consider</u> myself to be a decent player. Next month I <u>will compete</u> in the championships.

A Replace each underlined verb with a verb from the box. Use the correct tense to make the order of events clear. Write the paragraph.

tremble	develop	adore	erase	terrify	yearn

1. When I was younger, sports <u>scared</u> me. **2.** I <u>shook</u> when it was time for gym class. **3.** Now I <u>love</u> playing sports. **4.** I <u>want</u> to join the football team. **5.** Soon I <u>make</u> bigger muscles to get stronger. **6.** In a while, I <u>stop</u> all my doubts about participating in school sports.

B Add a verb of your own to complete each sentence. Then add a closing sentence. Write the paragraph.

7. Last year I _____ a new school. **8.** I _____ the choir to make new friends and learn how to sing. **9.** At first, I _____ like a frog. **10.** Now I _____ like a pro. **11.** My teacher even _____ my singing last month. **12.** Next month we _____ a recital for the entire school. **13.** I _____ not to be nervous. **14.** _____

C Write a paragraph about something you learned how to do. Compare how your skills were when you started and how they improved. Use correct verb tenses to make your writing clear.

Using Correct Verb Tenses

Use the correct verb tense to show action that is happening now **(present tense)**, action that happened in the past **(past tense)**, and action that will happen in the future **(future tense). Irregular verbs** do not end in **-ed** in the past tense. Memorize irregular verbs or use a dictionary.

Present: The honeybees <u>collect</u> nectar.
Past: Manny <u>moved</u> to Minnesota last year.
Future: He <u>will study</u> agriculture in college.

Some Irregular Verbs:

are/were	find/found	hear/heard	sing/sang
breed/bred	fly/flew	is/was	sleep/slept
bring/brought	give/gave	know/knew	take/took
catch/caught	go/went	make/made	think/thought
drive/drove	grow/grew	run/ran	throw/threw
eat/ate	have/had	see/saw	wear/wore

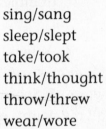

 Write the correct verb form in ( ) to complete each sentence.

1. Beekeepers who (live, will live) up north prepare the hives for winter.
2. Honeybees (are, were) always very sensitive to cold weather.
3. They (need, needed) to stay warm during winter.
4. Yesterday, beekeepers (wrapped, will wrap) the hives.
5. Paper and plastic (will protect, protected) the bees next winter.
6. These materials will (absorbed, absorb) the winter sun.

B Complete each sentence with a form of the verb in ( ). If necessary, change the verb so that it is in the correct tense. Write the sentences.

1. Last year, I (go) to a farm. **2.** I (see) many hard-working people. **3.** Early in the morning, I (milk) the cows. **4.** I knew that the animals (depend) on me. **5.** I (give) the animals water and food. **6.** I (visit) the farm again next year. **7.** When I visit, I (bring) a camera. **8.** Maybe I (stay) longer next time.

C Write a complete sentence using each verb in the tense given.

9. the present tense of *love*

10. the past tense of *believe*

11. the future tense of *like*

12. the past tense of *think*

13. the past tense of *sleep*

14. the future tense of *bring*

15. the present tense of *understand*

16. the past tense of *drive*

17. the present tense of *throw*

18. the future tense of *complain*

19. the past tense of *see*

20. the present tense of *cry*

21. the past tense of *catch*

22. the future tense of *play*

Review and Assess

Write the correct verb form in ( ) to complete each sentence.

1. Last year, Barry (breed, bred) bunnies in his backyard.
2. Next year, Rhonda (raise, will raise) roosters and rabbits.
3. Today, Hal (has, had) hundreds of hamsters.
4. Pedro (give, gave) water to all the ferrets yesterday morning.
5. Ken (keep, kept) gerbils in his room until his mother found out!
6. Jenna (take, took) care of the gerbils yesterday.

Write the letter of the verb that correctly completes each sentence.

7. I _____ all sorts of animals.

   A like   **C** likes
   B liking   **D** will like

8. Last month, I _____ a rabbit.

   A find   **C** finds
   B found   **D** will find

9. He _____ his whiskers when I fed him this morning.

   A will twitch   **C** twitches
   B twitching   **D** twitched

10. Yesterday, I _____ a gerbil to keep him company.

    A buys   **C** will buy
    B buy   **D** bought

11. Soon my room _____ like a zoo.

    A will seem   **C** seemed
    B seems   **D** seem

Replacing Dull Verbs

Avoid repeating verbs such as *say, go,* and *get*. These verbs can make your writing sound dull. Replace dull verbs with more vivid ones.

- The caterpillar <u>went</u> along the branch. Then it <u>went</u> into a ball.
- The caterpillar <u>crept</u> along the branch. Then it <u>curled</u> into a ball.

A Choose a word from the box to replace each underlined word. Write the verb tense correctly.

> **Words for *say/said:*** ask, shout, express, suggest
> **Words for *go/went:*** shot, march, dash, hurry

1. Yesterday, my teacher <u>said</u> how bees are similar to many animals. **2.** He <u>went</u> to the chalkboard and drew a bee and a bird. **3.** He asked us to <u>say</u> our thoughts about their similarities. **4.** My hand <u>went</u> up. **5.** Several other students loudly <u>said</u> answers. **6.** One student <u>said</u> that bees and birds both fly.

B Replace the underlined verb with a strong verb of your own. Write the verbs you choose.

7. Cats <u>go</u> on four legs. **8.** Mice <u>go</u> on four legs too. **9.** Cats often <u>get</u> mice. **10.** Last night, a mouse <u>went</u> across the room. **11.** My cat <u>went</u> after it. **12.** But the mouse <u>went</u> away. **13.** One day my cat will <u>get</u> that little mouse.

C Write a short essay that compares and contrasts two different animals. Replace dull verbs such as *say, go,* and *get* with vivid verbs.

Contractions

A **contraction** is a word made by combining two words. An **apostrophe** (')
shows where letters have been left out.

Many contractions are formed by joining a verb and *not*. An apostrophe
takes the place of *o* in *not*. There is only one contraction that includes a
spelling change: *will not* becomes *won't*.

I <u>do not</u> care.   I <u>don't</u> care.

They <u>will not</u> work.   They <u>won't</u> work.

Other contractions are formed by joining a pronoun and a verb.

<u>I am</u> so happy that <u>she is</u> coming.   <u>I'm</u> so happy that <u>she's</u> coming.

 Match a pair of words on the left with the correct contraction on the right.

1. I will	**A** didn't		
2. they are	**B** who'll		
3. we have	**C** I'll		
4. did not	**D** could've		
5. you have	**E** won't		
6. I am	**F** they're		
7. does not	**G** you've		
8. could have	**H** we've		
9. who will	**I** doesn't		
10. will not	**J** I'm		

Write the two words that make up each contraction.

11. What's that on the floor?

12. Animals don't talk!

13. That'll be the day.

14. You've never met my pig, Stinky.

15. He's fluent in many languages!

B Use contractions to replace the underlined words. Write the paragraph.

    1. Animals <u>do not</u> talk, but they do communicate. **2.** <u>They are</u> able to use sounds that have specific meanings. **3.** For instance, my dog barks when <u>he is</u> frightened. **4.** <u>I have</u> heard that monkeys are very intelligent. **5.** They <u>can not</u> talk, but they are able to recognize certain words and symbols. **6.** <u>We have</u> learned a lot about humans by studying monkeys. **7.** <u>That is</u> because monkeys and humans are actually quite similar. **8.** Of course, <u>we are</u> more intelligent than monkeys. **9.** People are able to form complete sentences, while monkeys <u>are not</u> able to do more than make their own sounds. **10.** But that <u>does not</u> mean that we can't learn about communication by studying monkeys.

C Combine each pronoun on the left with a word on the right to form a contraction. Write a sentence for each contraction that you form.

Pronouns

11. I	will
12. you	are
13. he	had
14. she	have
15. it	am
16. we	is
17. they	

Review and Assess

Write each pair of words as a contraction.

1. have not
2. must have
3. they are
4. we would
5. she is
6. we will
7. I would

Write the letter of the contraction that correctly completes each sentence.

8. _____ Emily's sister, right?

    A Your   **C** You're

    B Youre   **D** You'are

9. _____ right, I am.

    A Thats   **C** Thats'

    B That's   **D** That'll

10. I see _____ got something in common.

    A we've   **C** weve'

    B weve   **D** we'd

11. Yes, _____ got a dog like mine.

    A you   **C** youve

    B you've   **D** youv'e

12. _____ got to wash Fritz today.

    A Ive   **C** I've

    B Iv'e   **D** Ive'

Using Contractions in Informal Writing

You can use contractions to capture an informal, conversational voice.

- Since we <u>do not</u> have school today, <u>let us</u> go to a movie. (too formal)
- Since we <u>don't</u> have school today, <u>let's</u> go to a movie. (conversational)

A Use contractions to make this informal essay more conversational. Rewrite the essay.

    1. <u>We are</u> supposed to write about a funny pet. **2.** Well, <u>here is</u> my candidate. **3.** <u>It is</u> Sniffy, the food hound. **4.** We used to have a cocker spaniel who <u>did not</u> misbehave. **5.** Now we have a dog <u>who is</u> in trouble all the time. **6.** <u>He has</u> eaten a whole cherry pie. **7.** You <u>will not</u> believe this, but once he ate a pizza—cardboard, bag, and all! **8.** He <u>does not</u> even get sick. **9.** Mom says, "Sniffy <u>is not</u> a bad dog, just a hungry dog." **10.** We <u>would not</u> trade Sniffy for anything, but we do put food away now.

B Write a contraction to begin each sentence. Then complete the final sentence by explaining your own choice for a pet.

11. _____ never owned a ferret, but I hear they are interesting pets.
12. _____ cats easy to care for?
13. _____ a snake be an interesting pet?
14. _____ rather own a (name a pet) because _____.

C Write a paragraph that compares and contrasts two pets. Use details and contractions to develop a conversational voice.

Writing a Comparison/ Contrast Essay

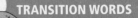

TRANSITION WORDS

Use transition words such as *similarly, however,* and *but* to signal likenesses and differences.

A **test** may ask you to write a comparison/contrast essay. Choose subjects that are alike and different. Follow the tips below.

Understand the prompt. Make sure you know what to do. Read the prompt carefully. A prompt for a comparison/contrast essay could look like this:

> **Compare and contrast two story characters in terms of how they try to solve a problem. Include important similarities and differences between the characters' efforts.**

Key words are *compare, contrast, characters, similarities,* and *differences.*

Find a good topic. Think of stories you have read recently in which the characters faced problems. Then choose two characters who are both similar and different.

Organize your ideas. Fill in a chart like the one below to organize the characters' likenesses and differences.

How are their efforts to solve problems similar?	Even though Mark is unhappy, he decides to give his new school a chance.	Even though Lupe is frustrated by sports, she decides to try playing marbles.
How do their efforts to solve problems differ?	Mark's first reaction is to go back to Vermont.	Lupe is determined to succeed.
How well does each solve the problem?	Mark becomes accepted after showing his basketball skills.	Lupe wins a trophy for being a great marbles player.

Write a good beginning. Write a strong topic sentence.

Develop and elaborate ideas. Use your comparison/contrast chart to organize your information.

Write a strong ending. Use the ending to sum up your thoughts.

Check your work. Ask a classmate to check your writing.

See how the essay below addresses the prompt, has a strong beginning, and uses the chart to remain focused on the topic.

Two Characters and Their Problems

1 — Lupe, in "The Marble Champ," and Mark, in "Going with the Flow," both face interesting challenges. Mark is bothered because he is the new kid in school. It doesn't help that he is deaf, either. — 2
Similarly, Lupe is upset because she's no good at sports.

3 — But the two characters are very different. When Mark faces a problem, he wants to flee back to his old school. As the newcomer, he knows he'll have to prove himself. After he displays his — 4
basketball skills, he finds that things improve. Lupe, on the other hand, succeeds at just about anything as long as it's not sports. She already has friends in school. However, she insists on succeeding at a sport. Finally, she becomes the marbles champ.

I think that Mark's problem was more difficult to solve because he also had a physical challenge. Even though they faced very different obstacles, Mark and Lupe both overcame their — 5
problems by working hard to solve them.

---

1. The first sentence explains what will be compared.
2. The writer forms contractions properly.
3. Transition words are used effectively.
4. Specific verbs make the writing clear.
5. This strong ending sums up the essay.

Adjectives

An **adjective** describes a noun or a pronoun. Many adjectives come before the words they describe. Adjectives can tell what kind, how many, or which one.

- **What kind:** We ate a <u>huge</u> turkey.
- **How many:** Dad ate <u>three</u> servings.
- **Which one:** <u>This</u> Thanksgiving was special.

The words **a, an**, and **the** are called **articles.** Articles are used before nouns or before words that modify, or describe, nouns.

- Use **a** before singular words that begin with a consonant sound:

  <u>a</u> turkey; <u>a</u> wonderful cook

- Use **an** before singular words that begin with a vowel sound or a silent **h:**

  <u>an</u> egg; <u>an</u> honest answer

- Use **the** before singular or plural words beginning with any letter:

  <u>the</u> plate; <u>the</u> dishes

An adjective formed from a proper noun is a **proper adjective.** Proper adjectives are capitalized.

<u>Greek</u> music   <u>Spanish</u> olives

 A Read each sentence. Write **kind, many,** or **which** to tell if the underlined adjective answers the question *What kind? How many?* or *Which one?*

1. The United States has <u>several</u> important holidays.
2. My family invited <u>twenty</u> people to our Thanksgiving dinner.
3. <u>Other</u> U.S. holidays include Independence Day and Labor Day.
4. Which is your <u>favorite</u> holiday?
5. Is United Nations Day celebrated <u>this</u> month?

B Choose the article that makes sense in each sentence. Write the sentences.

1. Lina's father is (a, an) skilled cook.
2. He uses (a, an) interesting combination of ingredients.
3. Lina keeps him company in (the, an) kitchen.
4. She always lends her father (a, the) hand.
5. Tonight she prepares (a, an) delicious dish of spaghetti all by herself.
6. Her brother sets (the, an) table.
7. Everyone compliments Lina on how tasty (a, the) spaghetti is.
8. She replies that it's (a, an) honor to cook for them.
9. Lina is embarrassed by (an, the) attention.
10. She is thrilled that she has such (a, an) fine talent.

C Complete each sentence with an adjective of your own. Write the sentences.

11. Sharon works in a _____ hospital.
12. She works _____ day from 9 to 5.
13. She is married and has _____ children.
14. One of her children is a _____ cellist.
15. Arnold plays _____ music.
16. He has performed in _____ concerts.
17. He plays a very _____ cello.
18. It was made by a _____ craftsperson.
19. _____ old cellos are valuable.
20. Arnold handles the cello with _____ care.

UNIT 4 GRAMMAR

Review and Assess

Write each sentence. Underline the articles. Circle the adjectives.

1. Have you ever eaten a cookie in a Chinese restaurant?
2. Chinese restaurants give you one or two cookies after a meal.
3. Paul's favorite cookie is covered with crunchy almonds.
4. Many cookies include funny fortunes or lucky numbers.
5. Most people think the cookies come from China.
6. Actually, these cookies are produced in the United States.

Write the letter of the adjective in each sentence.

7. Chinese food is often cooked in a big pan called a wok. **8.** The food is cooked quickly over high heat. **9.** Dishes are usually completed within a few minutes. **10.** Chinese cooks often use many tasty vegetables in their dishes. **11.** They also like to prepare fresh fish. **12.** Chinese cuisine is filled with unique foods.

7. **A** food **C** big
   B often **D** pan

8. **A** food **C** quickly
   B cooked **D** high

9. **A** few **C** within
   B completed **D** dishes

10. **A** cooks **C** tasty
    B often **D** vegetables

11. **A** also **C** prepare
    B like **D** fresh

12. **A** cuisine **C** filled
    B unique **D** foods

Using Clear Adjectives in a How-to Report

Use adjectives to make your directions clear to your reader.

- You need to do a <u>few</u> things to have a <u>great</u> party. The <u>first</u> step is to invite your <u>favorite</u> friends. Then make sure you have <u>enough</u> food for them to eat. You also want to prepare <u>some</u> games to keep everyone entertained.

A Choose adjectives from the box to complete each sentence. Then write the paragraph.

> enough   several   complete   each   colorful   danceable

    1. Follow _____ step to throw a great party. **2.** First, make sure you have plenty of _____ music ready. **3.** Prepare _____ types of food so that everyone will have something to eat. **4.** Make _____ food for everybody. **5.** Now hang some _____ decorations around the room. **6.** Give each guest _____ directions to your house.

B Think about a game that you can play at a party. Write a sentence to answer each question below. Circle the adjectives you use.

    7. How many people do you need to play the game?
    8. How long does the game take to play?
    9. What materials do you need to play the game?
  10. How does the game begin?
  11. How is the winner declared?

C Write a how-to paragraph that explains how to play the game you described in Exercise B. Remember to include opening and closing sentences. Include adjectives to make the directions clear.

Using Adjectives to Improve Sentences

An **adjective** describes a noun or a pronoun. Use adjectives to add descriptive details so readers can picture what you are writing about. Make sure you do not use too many adjectives.

- **Lacks detail:** The boy won the race.
- **Adjectives add detail:** The <u>determined</u> boy won the <u>difficult</u> race.
- **Too many adjectives:** The <u>strong, determined, brave</u> boy won the <u>long, difficult, hard</u> race.

A Choose the better adjective in ( ) to add a descriptive detail to each sentence. Write the adjective you choose.

1. Alaska is a (large, happy) state.
2. However, it has a (sleepy, small) population.
3. Much of Alaska's (big, breathtaking) land is not developed.
4. Wildlife roam the (brown, rugged) mountains.
5. (Beautiful, nice) meadows have many grazing animals.
6. (Some, Threatening) clouds tell of a coming snowstorm.

The following sentences have too many adjectives. Choose one of the underlined adjectives in each sentence. Write each sentence, using the adjective you choose.

7. The <u>quick, fast, speedy</u> sled sped over the icy trail.
8. <u>Towering, tall, majestic</u> mountains loomed in the distance.
9. Olga shivered in the <u>icy, frigid, chilly</u> air.
10. She stopped for a <u>quick, short, brief</u> rest.
11. Then she set off again on her <u>sturdy, rugged, strong</u> sled.

B Replace each underlined adjective with a more vivid or precise adjective. Write the sentences.

1. Suki barked at the <u>big</u> trees.
2. Heavy snow bent the <u>little</u> branches.
3. Henry pulled on his <u>nice</u> dog's leash.
4. "Suki," he sighed, "those are only <u>regular</u> trees."
5. The boy and his <u>good</u> pet continued quietly.
6. Suddenly, Henry heard a <u>loud</u> sound.
7. Suki's <u>good</u> ears stood up.
8. The <u>loud</u> sound grew more intense.
9. Henry realized there was a <u>large</u> avalanche.
10. Suki and Henry raced down the <u>cold</u> path.

C Add two adjectives to make each sentence clear. Write the new sentences.

11. _____ people stood by the side of the _____ trail.
12. _____ sleds pulled by _____ dogs rushed by.
13. The _____ crowd waved banners and _____ flags.
14. The winner was blanketed with a _____ wreath of _____ flowers.
15. He celebrated by throwing his _____ gloves into the _____ air.
16. Then he gave a _____ speech and thanked his _____ assistants.
17. A _____ snowball fight erupted as the band struck up a _____ tune.
18. The _____ dogs were unleashed and given _____ treats.
19. The _____ contestants were led on a _____ parade through town.
20. They trudged through the _____ snow with _____ smiles on their faces.

Review and Assess

Choose the better adjective in ( ) that adds vivid detail to each sentence. Write the sentences.

1. Long shadows stretched along the (white, moonlit) snow.
2. As it grew darker, Maurice slipped on the (cold, icy) path.
3. Maurice got up and rubbed his (throbbing, hurt) knee.
4. He walked gingerly along the rest of the (hard, treacherous) path.
5. When he got home, he took a (good, soothing) bath.

Write the letter of the adjective that adds the clearest or most vivid detail.

6. Many _____ dogs are well suited for living in cold climates. 7. Their _____ coats protect them from the chilly temperatures. 8. During _____ summer days, however, the heat makes their tongues hang out! 9. Give them as much _____ water as they want. 10. Let them take plenty of naps in the _____ shade.

6. A nice	C only	9. A blue	C refreshing
B funny	D furry	B wet	D white

7. A cold	C brown	10. A cool	C sleeping
B thick	D old	B loud	D falling

8. A few	C chilly
B icy	D scorching

Elaborating with Adjectives

Good writers use strong, specific adjectives to add clear details and information to a how-to report.

- Wear <u>appropriate</u> clothing when <u>extreme</u> weather comes your way. It would be pointless to wear a <u>bulky</u> parka on a <u>steamy</u> summer day. Would you think of wearing <u>teensy</u> shorts at the <u>frigid</u> North Pole?

A Make the sentences clearer by replacing each underlined adjective with a strong adjective from the box. Use each word once. Write the sentences.

straw	blistering	loose-fitting
protective	simple	dark

1. Dress carefully on a <u>hot</u> day in the summer.
2. First, choose sunglasses with <u>good</u> lenses to protect your eyes.
3. Wear a <u>light</u> hat with a wide brim to protect your face.
4. Put on a <u>big</u>, comfortable T-shirt.
5. Finally, you should apply <u>some</u> cream to block the sun's rays.
6. Follow these <u>good</u> tips to make it through the hottest days.

B Complete each sentence in the paragraph with a strong adjective of your own. Write the paragraph.

7. We have _____ winters here in Alaska. 8. I wear _____ socks and fur-lined boots. 9. I also wear _____ layers of clothing. 10. Underneath my clothing, I wear _____ underwear. 11. Last, I put on a _____ coat, a warm hat, and a pair of gloves. 12. I am always able to go out, even if there is a _____ blizzard.

C Write a how-to report about preparing for an extremely hot or cold day. Use specific adjectives to add strong details and liveliness to your report.

Comparative and Superlative Adjectives

Adjectives can compare people, places, or things. Adjectives change form when they are used to make comparisons.

- A **comparative adjective** compares two things or groups. Add **-er** to the end of most adjectives to make them comparative: smaller. Use **more** with long adjectives in the comparative form: more outstanding.

- A **superlative adjective** compares three or more things or groups. Add **-est** to the end of most adjectives to make them superlative: fastest. Use **most** with long adjectives in the superlative form: most incredible.

- For most adjectives that end with a **consonant** and **y,** change the **y** to **i** before you add **-er** or **-est:** happy, happier, happiest.

- For most one-syllable adjectives that end in a single consonant after a single vowel, double the final consonant before adding **-er** or **-est:** thin, thinner, thinnest.

- If an adjective ends with **e,** drop the final **e** before you add **-er** or **-est:** nice, nicer, nicest.

- Adjectives such as *good* and *bad* have **irregular** comparative and superlative forms: good, better, best; bad, worse, worst.

A   Write the correct adjective in ( ) to complete each sentence.

1. People say that the (wiser, wisest) animal of all is the owl. **2.** The woodpecker makes the (more annoying, most annoying) noise of any bird I know. **3.** The rabbit has (longer, longest) ears than the wolf. **4.** Are raccoons (more curious, most curious) animals than otters? **5.** The cheetah is the (better, best) runner of all.

B Copy the table below. Add **-er**, **-est**, **more**, or **most** to the adjectives in the first column. Complete the table.

Adjective	Comparative Adjective	Superlative Adjective
old	1.	2.
fine	3.	4.
flat	5.	6.
tall	7.	8.
lonely	9.	10.
wonderful	11.	12.
hot	13.	14.
bad	15.	16.
valuable	17.	18.
difficult	19.	20.

C Complete each sentence by writing the correct form of the adjective in ( ).

21. I read the (captivating) Native American tale of all.
22. Many of the (good) tales are about animals.
23. One tale told why an owl is the (smart) creature in the whole forest.
24. The (tricky) animal in many Native American tales is called Coyote.
25. Coyote is generally considered to be (intelligent) than other animals.

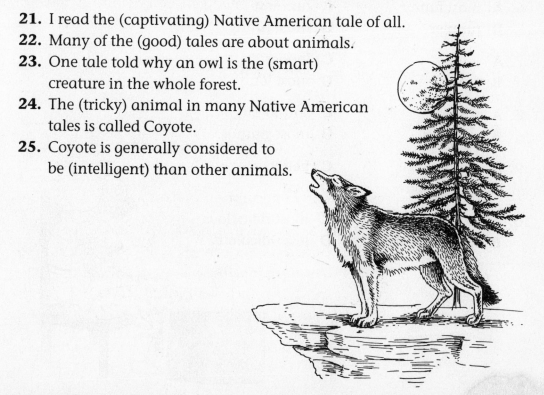

Review and Assess

Write the missing forms of the adjectives to complete the chart.

Adjective	Comparative	Superlative
1. dry		driest
2. understanding	more understanding	
3. mad		maddest
4. friendly		friendliest
5. fast	faster	

Write the letter of the word or words that complete each sentence.

6. Emily is the _____ member of her family. **7.** She has _____ hair than her sister. **8.** She also has the _____ ideas of all. **9.** Emily thinks that her left foot is her _____ feature. **10.** Isn't that the _____ thing that you have ever heard?

6. A most funny   **C** funniest
   B funnier   **D** more funny

7. A long   **C** longer
   B longest   **D** most long

8. A strange   **C** strangest
   B stranger   **D** most strange

9. A good   **C** better
   B more good   **D** best

10. A ridiculous   **C** most ridiculous
    B more ridiculous   **D** less ridiculous

Making Comparisons in a How-to Report

Use different forms of adjectives in your writing to provide your reader with precise instructions. Add comparative and superlative adjectives to make information in your how-to report clear.

- Even the <u>wildest</u> animal can learn how to behave. The <u>most successful</u> trainers are usually <u>more patient</u> than unsuccessful trainers.

A Use the correct form of the adjectives in ( ). Then write an opening sentence. Write the paragraph.

1. _____ **2.** I take care of my hamsters so they are the (happy) pets in the world. **3.** Every morning, I give them the (pure) bottled water I can find. **4.** I also buy the (tasty) food they sell at the pet shop. **5.** When I clean their cages, I do the (good) job possible. **6.** I think that hamsters are (wonderful) than dogs!

B Imagine you are a dog trainer who is explaining how to teach a dog to fetch. Add a different comparative or superlative adjective to complete each sentence. Then write a closing sentence.

7. Work in the _____ outdoor space you can find.
8. First, use your _____ tone of voice.
9. Then say "Fetch!" as you throw the _____ ball you can find.
10. Next, throw the ball _____ than you did before.
11. Remember that some dogs find it _____ to sit than to fetch!
12. Afterward, give your dog the _____ hug you can.

C Write a paragraph that tells how to train or take care of an animal. Include comparative and superlative adjectives.

Adverbs

Adverbs can tell more about verbs. Adverbs can tell **how, when,** or **where** an action happens. An adverb can appear before or after the verb. Many adverbs that tell *how* end in **-ly.**

- **How:** Harriet <u>quickly</u> crossed the finish line. She won <u>easily</u>.
- **When:** Harriet ran <u>today</u>. She <u>rarely</u> runs on Fridays.
- **Where:** Harriet ran <u>outdoors</u>. She ran <u>far</u>.

Like adjectives, adverbs change form when they are used to make comparisons.

Add **-er** to an adverb when two actions are being compared. This is the **comparative form** of the adverb: Jim stayed <u>longer</u> than Billy.

Add **-est** when three or more actions are being compared. This is the **superlative form** of the adverb: Jane stayed <u>longest</u> of all.

Use **more** or **most**, instead of **-er** or **-est**, with most adverbs that end in **-ly.** Do not use **more** or **most** with **-er** and **-est** endings.

> **Comparative:** Hal ran <u>more quickly</u> than Walter did.
> **Superlative:** Larry ran <u>most quickly</u> of all.

The adverbs **well** and **badly** have special forms that show comparison:

Adverb: well   **Comparative:** better   **Superlative:** best
Adverb: badly   **Comparative:** worse   **Superlative:** worst

A   Write the adverb in each sentence. Then write the verb it tells more about.

1. Karen glanced briefly at her watch.
2. Her feet burned painfully in her running shoes.
3. This tired girl never had run in a marathon.
4. Karen relaxed and ran more slowly.

B Complete each sentence by choosing the correct adverb in ( ).
Write the adverbs you choose.

1. We jogged (more easily, most easily) than before.
2. We ran (steadily, most steadily) for an hour.
3. Larry runs (gracefully, more gracefully) than David does.
4. David runs (slower, slowly) around the track.
5. I ran (more slowly, most slowly) of all.
6. Rico arrived home (more soon, sooner) than anyone else.
7. He (greedily, more greedily) gulped down a quart of water.
8. When I reached the front door, I (most nearly, nearly) collapsed.
9. I recovered (most quickly, quickly) after drinking some juice.
10. Tomorrow I will run (better, best) than today.

C Complete each sentence by writing your own adverbs.

11. Owen _____ realized he was lost in the forest.
12. He sat _____ on the base of a large tree by a brook.
13. He _____ used his compass to get his bearings.
14. Then he _____ headed back to his parents' tent.
15. Owen called _____ to let his parents know he was back.
16. His parents waved _____ when they saw him approaching.
17. "We were getting worried about you," his Mom said _____.

Review and Assess

Write the adverb in each sentence.

1. Have you ever watched the Olympics?
2. The Olympics were held originally in Athens.
3. Most Olympic athletes train constantly.
4. They work hard to reach peak performance.
5. The world's athletes participate enthusiastically.

Write the letter of the correct answer to each question.

6. Which word is the comparative form of the adverb *long*?

    A longer   **C** more long

    B longest   **D** most long

7. Which word is the superlative form of the adverb *well*?

    A better   **C** more good

    B best   **D** most good

8. Which word is an adverb that tells when something happened?

    A slow   **C** now

    B beyond   **D** here

9. Which word is not an adverb?

    A quickly   **C** time

    B far   **D** often

10. Which word is a superlative adverb?

    A worst   **C** more difficult

    B badly   **D** harder

Using Adverbs to Show Time Order

A well-written how-to report clearly shows the order of steps. Use time-order adverbs such as *first, next,* and *finally* to help you.

- When you decide to run in a long-distance race, you need to make special preparations. <u>First</u>, practice running long distances for at least several weeks before the race. <u>Then</u> on the day of the race, wear comfortable clothing.

A Choose the correct adverb in ( ) for each sentence to clearly show the order of steps. Write the adverbs. Then write a closing sentence.

    1. Before running in a long-distance race, make sure you (then, first) run a few practice races. **2.** (Before, Then) arrive early and do plenty of stretching exercises. **3.** (First, Next), begin to run at a comfortable pace. **4.** (Now, During) make sure you drink plenty of fluids as you run. **5.** (First, Finally), as you approach the finish line, keep up your pace.
6. _____

B Put the sentences for this explanation of how to choose a baseball glove in order. Use several time-order adverbs. Add an opening and a closing sentence. Write the report.

    7. Make sure the glove fits your hand well. **8.** Pay for the glove at the cash register. **9.** Try several gloves and choose the one you like best. **10.** Decide which kind of glove you want. **11.** Go to a sporting goods store that has a wide selection of gloves.

C Imagine you want to teach a friend how to play your favorite sport. Write a paragraph that explains the steps. Use adverbs to make the order of steps clear.

Using Adverbs to Improve Sentences

Remember that **adverbs** can tell more about verbs. They tell **how, when,** or **where** actions happen. You can improve your sentences with adverbs. Use adverbs to add descriptive details so that readers can picture the action. Too many adverbs, however, can make a sentence confusing.

- **Original sentence:** Eduardo placed the photograph in the box.
- **Adverb adds detail:** Eduardo <u>gently</u> placed the photograph in the box.
- **Too many adverbs:** Eduardo <u>gently, carefully, and cautiously</u> placed the photograph in the box.

A Each sentence below uses too many adverbs. Choose one adverb from each sentence. Write the sentence using only that adverb.

   1. Dennis frequently visits Grandpa Joe often. **2.** When they are together, they normally, usually play card games. **3.** Occasionally, they take long walks in the park often. **4.** They talk quietly, softly to each other. **5.** Grandpa Joe carefully, thoughtfully, and slowly teaches Dennis about the animals and trees in the park. **6.** Dennis is incredibly, immensely, and extremely excited when he visits his grandfather.

Write an adverb from the box to add detail to each sentence.

joyfully	forever	there

   7. The memory album is displayed _____ on the table. (where)

   8. My happy family smiled _____ in the group photo. (how)

   9. This album is something we will treasure _____. (when)

B Write an adverb of your own to add detail to each sentence. The words in ( ) tell which kind of adverb to use.

1. I _____ enjoy fishing with Uncle Charlie. (when)
2. We sit _____ out there on the lake. (how)
3. We_____ go out on rainy days. (when)
4. Sometimes the little boat rocks _____ on the lake. (how)
5. I cast my line _____ and wait for a bite. (where)
6. The fish swim _____ below the surface. (how)
7. I reel in my line _____ when I feel a tug. (how)
8. Uncle Charlie leans _____ to help me land the fish. (where)

C Write an adverb to make each sentence more vivid.

9. _____ I traveled many hours to visit my relatives.
10. I _____ love visiting my relatives.
11. Grandma _____ gives me a big hug when I visit her.
12. Grandpa _____ tells stories about what life was like years ago.
13. We sit _____ by the fireplace and exchange stories.
14. _____ Grandpa talks about the years he spent in the Navy.
15. Everybody listens _____ to his stories about ships.

Review and Assess

Each sentence uses too many adverbs. Choose one adverb from each sentence. Write the sentence using only that adverb.

1. I was completely, totally, absolutely surprised when Grandfather handed me the present.
2. Then I immediately, quickly, rapidly opened the small package.
3. It was obviously, definitely, really a book, but the pages were blank!
4. "How come the pages are blank, Grandfather?" I asked unhappily, dejectedly, sadly.
5. "You can use the book to write down your memories," he cheerfully, excitedly, pleasantly replied.

Read the paragraph. Write the letter of the adverb from each sentence.

6. Some traditions are passed down orally. 7. Often traditions are presented through stories or tales. 8. People use tape recorders to clearly record their family's stories. 9. Usually a younger family member will interview an older family member. 10. Families certainly value these oral histories.

6. **A** Some   **C** passed
   B traditions   **D** orally

7. **A** Often   **C** tales
   B presented   **D** stories

8. **A** People   **C** record
   B recorders   **D** clearly

9. **A** interview   **C** family
   B will   **D** Usually

10. **A** oral   **C** value
    B certainly   **D** these

Describing Your Ideas Clearly

A how-to report should present ideas clearly. Often, readers are confused by misplaced modifiers. Keep your modifiers close to the words they modify, or describe. The first sentence below suggests that "we" are hidden in an old trunk. The second sentence rearranges the words to make the meaning clear.

- **Misplaced modifier:** <u>Hidden in an old trunk,</u> we found a leather photograph album.

- **Improved:** We found a leather photograph album hidden in an old trunk.

A Improve the how-to report by rearranging the underlined words in each sentence. Write the sentences.

1. Collect your memories by following these steps <u>in a photo journal</u>.
2. Collect photos in a neat pile <u>that you like</u>.
3. Put any pictures in a box <u>that you don't want</u>.
4. Paste the photos on the pages <u>that are your favorites</u>.
5. Place the photo on the cover <u>that you like best</u>.

B Rearrange the words in each sentence to fix misplaced modifiers. Then write two more sentences that use at least one descriptive adverb each.

6. Make a scrapbook to store newspaper clippings of cardboard.
7. You can find pieces of cardboard at a dry cleaner's that are the same size. 8. Buried in the back pages of the newspaper, you may find the best articles.

C Write a how-to report about something you can make to save memories. For example, explain how to make a scrapbook or a journal. Check your sentences to avoid misplaced modifiers.

Writing a How-to Report

A **test** may ask you to write a how-to report. Be sure to include all the steps. Remember to use time-order words such as *first* and *next* to show the order of steps. Follow the tips below.

VISUALIZE

As you write each step, picture yourself doing it. This will help you include all the information.

Understand the prompt. Make sure you know what to do. Read the prompt carefully. A prompt for a how-to report may look like this:

> **Write a report that gives steps on how to make or do something. Make your report interesting to read and easy to understand. Explain all the steps and materials needed.**

Key words and phrases are *report, how to make or do, steps,* and *materials.*

Find a good topic. Make a list of possible topics. Narrow your list by asking yourself these questions: What are the basic steps? What information should I include? Can I present the steps clearly?

Organize your ideas. Write a how-to chart on scratch paper. Write the name of your task, the materials needed, and a list of steps. Your chart might look like this:

Task:	Record family memories with a tape recorder.
Steps:	Gather materials (tape recorder, microphone, tape). Invite relatives to join the project. Ask them to share a memory or a story. Put cassette into tape player. Press PLAY and RECORD. Have family members speak clearly into microphone. Stop recording when done. Rewind cassette to beginning of tape. Store tape safely.

Write a good beginning. Write a catchy opening sentence.

Develop and elaborate ideas. Use your chart to help you organize the sequence of steps. Use time-order words to clearly show when to do each step.

Write a strong ending. Write a clear, strong conclusion.

Check your work. Proofread your work by reading it softly to "hear" errors.

See how the report below addresses the prompt; has a catchy beginning and a strong, clear ending; and stays focused on the topic.

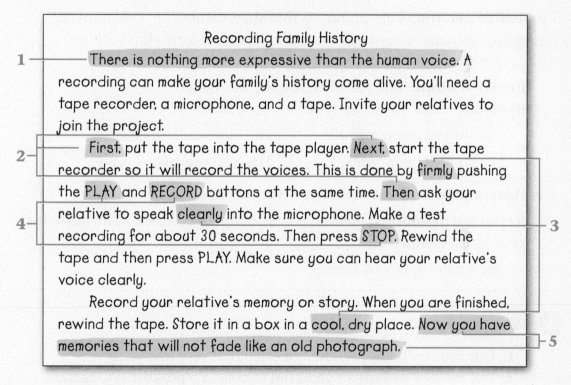

Recording Family History

1 — There is nothing more expressive than the human voice. A recording can make your family's history come alive. You'll need a tape recorder, a microphone, and a tape. Invite your relatives to join the project.

2 — First, put the tape into the tape player. Next, start the tape recorder so it will record the voices. This is done by firmly pushing the PLAY and RECORD buttons at the same time. Then ask your relative to speak clearly into the microphone. Make a test recording for about 30 seconds. Then press STOP. Rewind the tape and then press PLAY. Make sure you can hear your relative's voice clearly.

Record your relative's memory or story. When you are finished, rewind the tape. Store it in a box in a cool, dry place. Now you have memories that will not fade like an old photograph. — 5

1. The first sentence grabs the reader's attention.
2. The writer uses time-order words that show the order of steps.
3. The writer uses strong adverbs and adjectives to write clear sentences.
4. Special terms are given to make the process clear.
5. This strong ending sums up the writer's thoughts.

Pronouns

Pronouns replace nouns or noun phrases. *I, you, he, she, it, me, him,* and *her* are singular pronouns that replace singular nouns. *We, you, they, us,* and *them* are plural pronouns that replace a plural noun or compound nouns. The pronoun *I* is always capitalized.

Laura wanted to vote. Laura and Mai wanted to vote.
She wanted to vote. They wanted to vote.

Possessive pronouns are pronouns that show ownership. One form of possessive pronouns is used before nouns. The other form stands alone without a noun following it.

Before a noun: my, your, her, his, its, our, their
By itself: mine, yours, hers, his, its, ours, theirs

Lila studied women's rights. The idea was Franco's.
Lila studied their rights. The idea was his.

A **reflexive pronoun** usually refers to the subject of the sentence.

Reflexive pronouns: myself, yourself, himself, herself, itself, ourselves, yourselves, themselves

She waited in line by herself.

 A Write the pronoun in each sentence.

1. Our country holds presidential elections every four years.
2. You must be at least 18 years old to vote in a presidential election.
3. Candidates for President hold debates for us about important issues.
4. They also give speeches across the country.
5. A candidate will meet many voters in order to get their votes.
6. Voters must keep themselves informed about the issues.

B Write a pronoun in ( ) to replace each underlined noun or noun phrase.

1. Harry Andrews had a pile of newspapers and sold <u>newspapers</u> (him, them) to his customers. **2.** Harry got <u>the customers'</u> (their, its) attention by screaming the headlines. **3.** Some of <u>the people</u> (them, he) just ignored Harry. **4.** Other folks bought <u>Harry's</u> (theirs, his) newspapers each day. **5.** After they bought the papers, <u>Harry</u> (he, it) always thanked his customers. **6.** <u>Harry's</u> (Mine, His) favorite customer was Miss Johnson. **7.** She never failed to buy a newspaper and to greet <u>Harry</u> (him, her) with a smile. **8.** Harry thought <u>Miss Johnson</u> (you, she) was the nicest person in the whole city.

C Replace each underlined noun or noun phrase with a pronoun. Write the pronoun you choose.

9. Six clowns jumped out of a little car, and <u>the clowns</u> did magic tricks.

10. How could the clowns pack <u>the clowns</u> into that tiny car?

11. Paula and I came early. <u>Paula and I</u> waited for the bands to begin.

12. <u>Marching bands</u> passed by with drums banging out the music's beat.

13. <u>The music</u> was loud, and Paula and I cheered just as loudly.

14. <u>Paula and I</u> had never seen such a parade.

15. Later, I found a banner from the parade and gave it to <u>Paula</u>.

Review and Assess

Replace each underlined noun or noun phrase with a pronoun. Write the pronouns.

1. Erica is a smart girl. <u>Erica</u> loves politics and watching elections.
2. She follows all of <u>the elections</u> across the country.
3. Many of <u>Erica's</u> friends enjoy politics too.
4. <u>Erica, Louise, and Phil</u> discuss politics every day.
5. Erica shares her opinions with <u>Louise and Phil</u>.
6. Politics is a passion of <u>Erica's</u>.
7. Jay Taylor is Erica's favorite candidate, and she has met <u>Jay Taylor</u>.

Write the letter of the pronoun that completes each sentence.

8. Voters should keep _____ informed about the candidates.

    A he   **C** she
    B themselves   **D** ours

9. Read about different candidates and listen to _____ speeches on TV.

    A their   **C** them
    B they   **D** we

10. Each of _____ votes can make a difference.

    A me   **C** us
    B you   **D** our

11. Go into the voting booth and close _____ curtain.

    A it   **C** I
    B its   **D** they

12. Pull the lever to register _____ vote.

    A it   **C** your
    B you   **D** yours

Using Pronouns to Improve Your Style

A research report should sound clear and smooth. Sentences that are too long may be confusing or boring for your readers. Use pronouns to make your sentences less wordy.

- I admire doctors and nurses because <u>doctors and nurses</u> help people.
- I admire doctors and nurses because <u>they</u> help people.

A Use a pronoun to replace each underlined noun phrase. Add an opening sentence.

1. _____ **2.** My plan is to work in the field of aviation because <u>the field of aviation</u> is fascinating. **3.** I'll study how to be a pilot or a mechanic because <u>pilots and mechanics</u> have interesting jobs. **4.** My aunt is a pilot. <u>My aunt</u> went to special flight schools. **5.** She used a flight simulator, and <u>the flight simulator</u> showed her how to fly a plane. **6.** I asked <u>my aunt</u> if she enjoyed her work. **7.** <u>My aunt</u> said that <u>her work as a pilot</u> was rewarding.

B Add pronouns to make the writing smoother. Rewrite sentences **11** and **12** so they do not begin with *I*. Write the paragraph.

8. I want to teach history because I enjoy learning about the past and how people lived _____ lives. **9.** If possible, I would teach American history because _____ fascinates _____. **10.** I am particularly interested in George Washington and _____ efforts to form _____ country. **11.** I think _____ was a great President, and _____ life was incredible. **12.** I hope to be a great teacher for _____ students.

C Write a paragraph about the training you would need for a career that interests you. Remember that pronouns can keep your sentences from becoming too wordy.

Subject and Object Pronouns

Pronouns that are used as the subjects of sentences are **subject pronouns.**

> <u>We</u> learned about the term "Underground Railroad."

> <u>It</u> first appeared in print in the 1840s.

Singular subject pronouns: I, you, he, she, it

Plural subject pronouns: we, you, they

When you use a person's name and a pronoun in a **compound subject**, be sure to use a subject pronoun. When *I* is used with another pronoun or a noun, *I* comes last.

> Betty and <u>I</u> studied the Underground Railroad.

> <u>She</u> and <u>I</u> imagined following that route.

Pronouns that are used in the predicates of sentences are called **object pronouns.**

> Betty told <u>me</u> about Harriet Tubman. She read about <u>her</u>.

Singular object pronouns: me, you, him, her, it

Plural object pronouns: us, you, them

 Read each sentence. Write **S** if the underlined word is a subject pronoun. Write **O** if the word is an object pronoun.

1. Mr. Harris told <u>us</u> stories.
2. Then <u>we</u> made him tell them again.
3. <u>They</u> were exciting stories, and Mr. Harris told them well.
4. We often asked <u>him</u> to tell about the Civil Rights movement.
5. <u>It</u> was an important period in United States history.
6. <u>He</u> told us the story of Rosa Parks and segregation.
7. "Do you know how Rosa Parks helped <u>me</u>?" Mr. Harris asked.
8. "<u>She</u> gave me the strength to fight for freedom," Mr. Harris said.

B Write the correct pronoun in ( ) to complete each sentence.

1. Today my class and (I, me) learned about Harriet Tubman.
2. My teacher told (me, I) that Tubman helped runaway slaves.
3. Tubman helped (them, they) escape to the North, where slavery was illegal.
4. They followed (her, she) along the Underground Railroad.
5. The Underground Railroad was secret, and few records were kept of (it, them).
6. But many stories survive, and (them, they) tell about Tubman's work.
7. (Her, She) was courageous even though danger was everywhere.
8. My classmates and (I, me) were amazed by her story.

C Add a pronoun to complete each sentence. Write the pronouns.

9. My class and _____ went on a field trip.
10. Our teacher took _____ to the main library downtown.
11. We entered the library, and an elevator took _____ to the fourth floor.
12. _____ was a big elevator, and it held our whole group.
13. Some students wanted the elevator to take _____ to the top of the building!
14. _____ decided to get off with the rest of us, though.
15. Mr. Sutter, the librarian, was helpful, and _____ pointed out some good books.
16. Some were a few years old, but most of _____ were quite new.
17. I asked, "Mr. Sutter, would you help _____ find a book about Frederick Douglass?"
18. Then Mr. Sutter brought _____ several books.
19. I decided to borrow _____ all!

Review and Assess

Read each sentence. Write **S** if the underlined word is a subject pronoun. Write **O** if the word is an object pronoun.

1. I saw a man and asked <u>him</u> how to find the train station.
2. The man shrugged his shoulders and told <u>me</u> he did not know.
3. "<u>It</u> might be down the street," he said.
4. A nice woman overheard <u>us</u> and offered to show me to the station.
5. <u>I</u> thanked her when we got there.

Write the letter of the word that completes each sentence.

6. Derek asked Mike and _____ for directions.

   A I   **C** they
   B me   **D** he

7. We were glad to help _____.

   A I   **C** they
   B we   **D** him

8. _____ was catching a train.

   A Him   **C** Them
   B Her   **D** He

9. He thanked _____ and drove away.

   A us   **C** he
   B we   **D** they

10. We waved to _____ as he drove off.

    A I   **C** she
    B he   **D** him

Writing with Pronouns

In a research report, the information must be clear. Use the correct forms of pronouns so your readers are not confused or distracted.

- **Incorrect:** Harriet Tubman and Frederick Douglass are important figures in American history. Have you heard of <u>she and he</u>?

- **Correct:** Have you heard of <u>them</u>? Have you heard of <u>her and him</u>?

A Add the correct pronouns to make each sentence clear.

1. Let _____ tell you about Martin Luther King, Jr. **2.** _____ was a great man. **3.** On August 28, 1963, King delivered an important speech, and _____ will be remembered throughout history. **4.** King spoke about _____ four children. **5.** He dreamed that _____ would not be judged by the color of _____ skin. **6.** _____ speech had a dramatic impact on _____ all.

B Complete this paragraph about Harriet Tubman. First, write a pronoun for each numbered item. Then add words of your own to complete each sentence. The first one is done for you.

7. Harriet Tubman impresses <u>me</u> because <u>she risked her life for others</u>. **8.** _____ was born a slave _____. **9.** Although it was dangerous for _____, _____. **10.** Later, she helped other slaves as _____ tried to escape _____. **11.** She led _____ to freedom _____. **12.** I believe that _____ _____.

C Write a paragraph about one of your heroes. Check your writing to make sure that you use subject and object pronouns correctly.

Pronouns and Their Referents

Pronouns get their meaning from the nouns they replace. The noun or noun phrase that a pronoun replaces is called its **referent,** or antecedent. A pronoun and its referent must agree. In these sentences, the referents are underlined once, and the pronouns are underlined twice.

The hungry <u>bird</u> flew very low as <u><u>it</u></u> hunted for worms.

<u>Birds and some insects</u> are similar. <u><u>They</u></u> both are able to fly.

In the sentences above, the singular subject pronoun *it* agrees with its referent, *bird.* The plural subject pronoun *They* agrees with its referent, *Birds and some insects.*

 Write each sentence. Underline each pronoun. Circle each referent.

1. Greg and Abdul were glad when they arrived in Central Park.
2. The boys brought a kite and flew it all afternoon.
3. Then Greg and Abdul sat down and ate their picnic lunch.
4. Greg waved at the bike riders speeding past him.
5. Both boys napped as the sun warmed them.

Write a pronoun to replace each underlined noun or noun phrase.

6. Emily first went to New York City when <u>Emily</u> was eight years old. 7. Her favorite place to visit is the Empire State Building because <u>the Empire State Building</u> is so tall. 8. Tourists from around the world go to the observation deck. <u>Tourists</u> get a great view of New York City. 9. The people on the ground look incredibly small because <u>the people on the ground</u> are so far away! 10. Now Emily is excited because her parents are taking <u>Emily</u> to New York City again this summer.

B Write the correct pronoun to complete each sentence.

1. A chameleon can change _____ color and blend into the background.
2. Dogs tend to bark loudly when _____ want to scare off predators.
3. An armadillo has a thick, plated shell that _____ uses as armor.
4. Most birds simply fly away when something frightens _____.
5. Whales are so big. Do you think _____ need protection?
6. Do you know how my mom protects my sisters and _____?
7. She teaches us safety rules and makes us follow _____.

C Use these referents to write sentences with pronouns. Make sure the pronouns and their referents agree.

8. three silly geese
9. chirping cricket
10. Susan
11. tall buildings
12. turtle
13. New York City
14. children
15. Central Park
16. Mary, Janet, and Doreen
17. helicopters
18. Uncle Timo
19. buses and trains
20. many restaurants

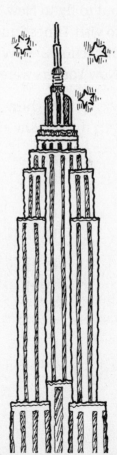

Review and Assess

Write the referent in each sentence that agrees with the underlined pronoun.

1. I asked a cricket if <u>it</u> would take a trip.
2. Then I heard a sharp click, and <u>it</u> startled me.
3. The cricket and I flew high. <u>We</u> soared through the clouds.
4. The clouds were puffy, and <u>they</u> filled the sky.
5. The trip was wonderful, even though <u>it</u> was just a dream.

Read the following paragraph. Write the letter of the pronoun that completes each sentence.

6. One morning, Chita combed her hair and put _____ in a neat bun.
7. Chita was about to fly to New York, and _____ wanted to look her best.
8. She planned to visit Times Square and City Hall because _____ were both popular tourist attractions. **9.** When she arrived in New York, Chita discovered that New Yorkers were very proud of _____ city.

6. A her   **C** him
   B it   **D** she

7. A us   **C** her
   B she   **D** its

8. A they   **C** her
   B them   **D** it

9. A him   **C** they
   B them   **D** their

Using Pronouns and Referents in Your Writing

Choose your words carefully when you write a research report. Make sure you use pronouns correctly so that your writing is clear and smooth. Check that the pronouns you use agree with their referents.

- The <u>city</u> seemed enormous to <u>Stan</u>. <u>It</u> frightened <u>him</u> just a bit.

A Change the underlined noun or noun phrase to a pronoun. Then write a closing sentence that uses at least one pronoun.

1. When people think of tall buildings, <u>people</u> often think of New York. **2.** New York has plenty of skyscrapers, but <u>New York</u> also has small buildings and several beautiful parks. **3.** The Statue of Liberty is a woman. <u>The woman</u> holds the torch of freedom. **4.** Years ago, ships brought immigrants to New York. Often the first thing <u>the immigrants</u> saw was the Statue of Liberty. **5.** The Statue of Liberty has a long flight of stairs inside. <u>The stairs</u> go right up to Lady Liberty's head. **6.** _____

B Write pronouns to complete each sentence. Then write a beginning sentence and a closing sentence that use pronouns. Write the paragraph.

7. _____ **8.** Native Americans lived in New York, and _____ were there when the Dutch came. **9.** When the Dutch arrived in New York, _____ soon became very crowded. **10.** People moved uptown when _____ downtown neighborhoods were too full. **11.** New York is still very crowded. Pedestrians have to watch _____ step or else they will bump into each other! **12.** New York and _____ citizens welcome visitors to the hustle and bustle. **13.** _____

C Write a short article with information about a big city that you know or have read about. Use pronouns to make your writing clear.

Prepositions and Prepositional Phrases

A **preposition** begins a group of words called a **prepositional phrase.** The noun or pronoun that follows the preposition is called the **object of the preposition.** Prepositional phrases can be used to tell more about the words they accompany.

- Emilio went <u>to</u> the embassy. (preposition)
- Emilio went <u>to the embassy</u>. (prepositional phrase)
- Emilio went to the <u>embassy</u>. (object of the preposition)

Common Prepositions				
about	around	between	into	to
above	at	by	of	under
across	behind	for	on	up
after	below	from	over	with
against	beneath	in	through	without

 A Write each sentence. Underline the prepositional phrase. Circle the preposition.

1. Emilio raced up the embassy steps.
2. The guard asked his name and showed Emilio to a large room.
3. The program began when the ambassador came into the room.
4. She smiled at her guests as she began her speech.
5. Later, Emilio realized how much he had learned about Japan.
6. He wrote a report for his history class.

B Write **P** if the underlined word is a preposition. Write **O** if it is the object of the preposition.

1. Have you ever been <u>to</u> the opera?
2. Last night they performed an opera under the <u>stars</u>.
3. People brought snacks and sat on <u>blankets</u>.
4. The concert began right <u>after</u> sunset.
5. The music continued <u>through</u> the night.
6. When the opera ended, people poured <u>into</u> the streets.

C Add a prepositional phrase of your own to complete each sentence. Write the sentence.

7. I live _____.
8. Each weekend I go _____.
9. I often look _____.
10. At the park, I climb _____.
11. After breakfast, I put my dishes _____.
12. When I get to school, I run right _____.
13. Then I put my book bag _____.
14. At lunchtime, I sit _____.
15. Then I bring my tray _____.
16. Sometimes I take my dog _____, and we play there.
17. Later, I hang his leash _____.
18. At bedtime, he jumps _____.

Review and Assess

Write the prepositional phrase in each sentence. Circle the preposition.

1. Larry left his passport in the house.
2. He was sure he had brought it with him.
3. He finally found the passport beneath magazines.
4. The ticket clerk looked closely at Larry's passport.
5. Then the clerk sent Larry to the waiting area.

Read the paragraph. Write the letter of the preposition that correctly completes each sentence.

6. *The Wizard of Oz* was released _____ 1939. **7.** The movie's main character, Dorothy, was played _____ Judy Garland. **8.** A twister carries Dorothy _____ the magical land of Oz, where she meets a tin man, a scarecrow, and a cowardly lion. **9.** Dorothy must follow a yellow brick road _____ the woods. **10.** _____ a series of adventures, Dorothy finally returns home.

6. **A** in   **C** over
   B on   **D** under

7. **A** in   **C** by
   B over   **D** through

8. **A** on   **C** at
   B to   **D** after

9. **A** through   **C** without
   B after   **D** with

10. **A** To   **C** Below
    B With   **D** After

Using Prepositional Phrases to Add Details

A research report presents a collection of facts and details. Prepositional phrases can provide important information to make your report interesting for your readers.

- Every town has people who work in the community <u>without pay</u>.

A Write a preposition to complete the prepositional phrase in each sentence.

    1. Mr. Chew came to our community _____ 1997.
    2. He runs a community center where children play _____ school.
    3. The center is located _____ the school athletic field.
    4. Before the center opened, we played _____ our yards.
    5. Now kids can play _____ each other in a safe place.
    6. It's great to have this center _____ our town.
    7. Where would our community be _____ Mr. Chew?

B Add information to each sentence by writing a prepositional phrase. Then write a closing sentence that uses a prepositional phrase.

    8. Every day when I walk _____ I pass the fire station.
    9. The volunteer firefighters often wave _____.
    10. When there is a fire _____, they jump into their fire trucks.
    11. The fire trucks race _____ amid the roar of sirens.
    12. As they speed _____, the firefighters prepare for the fire.
    13. They must always be ready _____.
    14. _____ the firefighters are usually exhausted.
    15. Each year, everyone gathers _____ to honor these brave workers.
    16. _____

C Write a paragraph about someone you admire who helps people in your community. Use prepositional phrases to add important details.

Conjunctions

Conjunctions such as *and, but,* and *or* can connect individual words, groups of words, or entire sentences. Conjunctions may be used to make compound subjects, compound predicates, and compound sentences. In compound sentences, you usually add a comma before the conjunction.

The conjunction you use depends on your purpose.

- Use *and* to join related ideas: His horse was fast <u>and</u> strong.
- Use *but* to join contrasting ideas: Some men escaped, <u>but</u> Paul Revere was captured.
- Use *or* to suggest a choice: Will you ride this horse <u>or</u> that horse?

Compound subject: <u>John Adams and George Washington</u> helped lead the American Revolution.

Compound predicate: Washington <u>led his troops and fought bravely</u>.

Compound sentence: <u>Revere was mainly a silversmith, but he was also a dentist.</u>

 Write the conjunction in each sentence.

1. The British and the colonists fought each other in the revolution.
2. King George III attempted to tax the colonists, but they rebelled.
3. Some people debated whether to be faithful to England or to fight.
4. The fighting was furious, but the colonists prevailed.
5. The colonists were victorious, and they won their independence.

Write the correct conjunction in ( ) to complete each sentence.

6. Revere (and, but) Adams were heroes of the American Revolution.
7. Revere rode a horse, (but, or) he did not reach Concord.
8. The young silversmith rode hard (and, but) fast.

B Use the conjunction *and, but,* or *or* to join each pair of sentences.
Write the sentences. Remember to add a comma.

1. Would you like to visit New York? Would you prefer to visit Boston?
2. Boston is a big city. New York City has more people.
3. Boston is an old city. New York City is old as well.
4. Boston has many universities. It is filled with thousands of students.
5. Many people apply to Harvard University. Only a few get in.
6. Young scientists might choose MIT. They might choose Harvard.
7. Boston has tall buildings. None is taller than the John Hancock Tower.
8. You can spend a day in Boston. You can spend a lifetime there.
9. Boston has many buses. The trains are faster.
10. You might want to take a bus. You might want to take a train.

C Read each group of words. Add more information and the conjunction
in ( ) to create a new sentence. Write the sentences.

11. visit battlefields of the American Revolution (or)
12. I want to learn more about the battles (and)
13. I have read about the battles (but)
14. see the Liberty Bell in Philadelphia (and)
15. there are many historic sites (but)
16. travel by car with my family (or)
17. so many things to do (and)
18. my favorite period in history
    is the American Revolution (but)

Review and Assess

Choose the conjunction *and, but,* or *or* to complete each sentence. Write the conjunction you use.

1. Charlie _____ Mary live on a farm. (and, but)
2. Charlie's horse is big, _____ Mary's horse is bigger. (but, or)
3. Did Mary ride a horse, _____ did she ride a pony? (but, or)
4. Ponies are small, _____ children enjoy riding them. (and, or)
5. Mary often rides ponies, _____ she prefers to ride horses. (and, but)

Write the letter of the word that best completes each sentence.

6. Henry Wadsworth Longfellow wrote hundreds of poems, _____ without a doubt one of his most famous poems is *Paul Revere's Ride*. **7.** Longfellow was known to be very kind, _____ he always had time to help other people. **8.** During his lifetime, Longfellow's poems were incredibly popular, _____ they are not as popular today. **9.** Longfellow wrote this famous poem, _____ it has brought American history to life.

6. **A** also   **C** or
   B anyway   **D** but

7. **A** and   **C** or
   B but   **D** while

8. **A** now   **C** but
   B and   **D** or

9. **A** and   **C** but
   B even   **D** or

Using Conjunctions in a Research Report

Avoid writing sentences that are all the same length. Short, direct sentences are useful, but too many short, choppy sentences in a row can become boring. Combine choppy sentences with conjunctions to make your writing flow smoothly.

- **Choppy:** Cars are fast. Planes are faster. They are just as safe.
- **Better:** Cars are fast, but planes are faster and just as safe.

A Complete each sentence by adding a conjunction.

   1. Wilbur _____ Orville Wright made history in 1903. **2.** They flew the first powered flight that carried humans, _____ their flight lasted only 59 seconds. **3.** The first plane traveled 852 feet, _____ about the length of three football fields. **4.** The first successful jet engine was made in 1939, _____ since then flying has never been the same. **5.** Today you can fly around the globe, _____ flight would not have been possible without the pioneering efforts of the Wright brothers.

B Combine the short sentences below to make the paragraph flow smoothly. Finish the last sentence by adding a conjunction and more information. Write the new paragraph.

   6. The earliest cars were slow. They often broke down. **7.** People worked to make cars more reliable. Soon cars broke down less often. **8.** Many cars today are very fuel-efficient. They still cause pollution. **9.** Cars in the future may use hydrogen power. They may use solar power. **10.** I look forward to new developments in automotive technology, _____.

C Write a paragraph about a type of transportation and how it has changed over time. Include conjunctions in your paragraph to make your sentences flow smoothly.

Writing a Summary

Some **tests** may ask you to summarize information from a graph, time line, or chart. You will need to read the information carefully and use it to develop your own sentences.

TIME LINES

Time lines give much information in few words. To summarize this information, fill in words to express complete ideas.

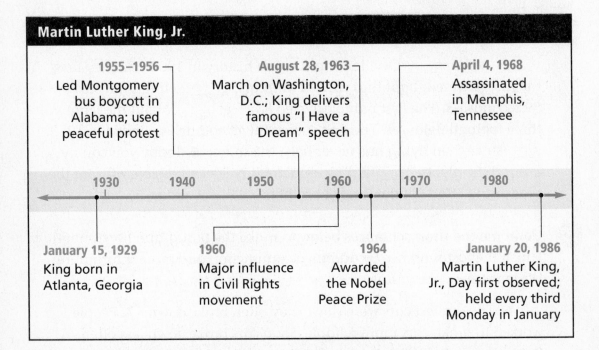

Martin Luther King, Jr.

1955–1956
Led Montgomery bus boycott in Alabama; used peaceful protest

August 28, 1963
March on Washington, D.C.; King delivers famous "I Have a Dream" speech

April 4, 1968
Assassinated in Memphis, Tennessee

1930   1940   1950   1960   1970   1980

January 15, 1929
King born in Atlanta, Georgia

1960
Major influence in Civil Rights movement

1964
Awarded the Nobel Peace Prize

January 20, 1986
Martin Luther King, Jr., Day first observed; held every third Monday in January

Organize your ideas. In a time line, information will already be arranged in order. In a chart or diagram, you will need to decide how to present information. In any case, you must put words into complete sentences and provide a beginning and a conclusion.

Write a good beginning. Think of a topic sentence that states the main idea you want to present about your subject.

Develop and elaborate ideas. Include all important details from the time line. Make sure the details support your main idea.

Write a strong ending. Try to write a "clincher" sentence to provide a clear ending. You might add a final comment of your own.

Check your work. Ask a classmate to read your summary. Are there places that need more details or clearer information? Are events in the proper order?

See how the summary below is based on information from the time line, along with the writer's own comments and ideas.

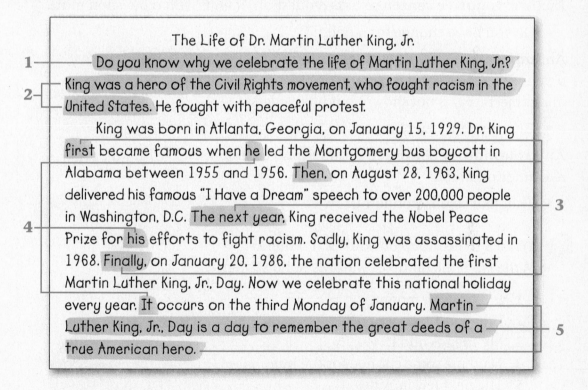

The Life of Dr. Martin Luther King, Jr.

1 — Do you know why we celebrate the life of Martin Luther King, Jr.?

2 — King was a hero of the Civil Rights movement, who fought racism in the United States. He fought with peaceful protest.

King was born in Atlanta, Georgia, on January 15, 1929. Dr. King first became famous when he led the Montgomery bus boycott in Alabama between 1955 and 1956. Then, on August 28, 1963, King delivered his famous "I Have a Dream" speech to over 200,000 people in Washington, D.C. The next year, King received the Nobel Peace Prize for his efforts to fight racism. Sadly, King was assassinated in 1968. Finally, on January 20, 1986, the nation celebrated the first Martin Luther King, Jr., Day. Now we celebrate this national holiday every year. It occurs on the third Monday of January. Martin Luther King, Jr., Day is a day to remember the great deeds of a true American hero.

1. This sentence engages readers with a question.
2. This sentence states the main idea.
3. The writer uses clue words to clearly show the order of events.
4. The use of pronouns avoids repeating words.
5. This ending returns to the main idea and reveals the writer's voice.

Review of Sentences

A **sentence** is a group of words that may be a statement, a question, a command, a request, or an exclamation. It begins with a capital letter and ends with a punctuation mark. A sentence always expresses a complete thought.

A **declarative sentence** makes a statement. It ends with a period.

- One dollar is equal to one hundred pennies**.**

An **interrogative sentence** asks a question. It ends with a question mark.

- Do you have change for a dollar**?**

An **imperative sentence** gives a command or a request. It ends with a period. The first word is usually a verb or *please* followed by a verb. The subject *(you)* is not shown, but it is understood.

- Give me that loaf of bread**.**

An **exclamatory sentence** shows strong feeling. It ends with an exclamation mark.

- That loaf smells wonderful**!**

 A Write **S** if the group of words is a sentence.
Write **NS** if the group of words is not a sentence.

1. Is too much money.
2. How much can you afford?
3. My friends and I.
4. Lend me some change for the bus.
5. The next few minutes.
6. That's really soon!
7. The express or another bus?
8. The express will get you there faster.

B Identify each sentence. Write **D** if it is a declarative sentence. Write **IN** if it is an interrogative sentence. Write **IM** if it is an imperative sentence. Write **E** if it is an exclamatory sentence.

1. Do you know much about the history of money? **2.** I think it is really fascinating. **3.** Tell me all about it. **4.** Coins were made from precious metals. **5.** When was paper money first used? **6.** Wow, that's a really good question! **7.** Ask your teacher. **8.** Do you mean that I should ask Ms. Lopez? **9.** Yes, she's an expert on everything. **10.** Do you think money will be around forever? **11.** I'm not sure. **12.** I wish I had more money! **13.** We all wish we had more money.

C Add words, capital letters, and punctuation marks to make each group of words the kind of sentence shown in ( ). Write the sentences.

14. what should we (interrogative)
15. to the stamp store (imperative)
16. a great store (exclamatory)
17. remarkable stamp collection (exclamatory)
18. stamps from all over the world (declarative)
19. they are valuable (interrogative)
20. worth ten dollars (exclamatory)
21. show (imperative)
22. my album from that table (imperative)
23. go to the stamp fair next week (interrogative)
24. a great idea (exclamatory)
25. Marta and Jimmy come too (interrogative)
26. love collecting stamps (declarative)
27. is the best hobby (exclamatory)

Review and Assess

Rewrite each sentence with correct capitalization and end punctuation.

1. did you go to the play last night
2. what a magical performance it was
3. the play lasted two hours
4. tell me all about it
5. who was the best actor
6. Ivan was fantastic
7. what role did he play
8. he played a detective

Write the letter of the words that tell what kind of sentence it is.

9. I will try out for the school play.

    A declarative sentence   **C** imperative sentence
    B exclamatory sentence   **D** interrogative sentence

10. Do I really want to stand in front of an audience?

    A declarative sentence   **C** imperative sentence
    B exclamatory sentence   **D** interrogative sentence

11. It can be scary performing in front of total strangers.

    A declarative sentence   **C** imperative sentence
    B exclamatory sentence   **D** interrogative sentence

12. Give it your best shot.

    A declarative sentence   **C** imperative sentence
    B exclamatory sentence   **D** interrogative sentence

13. I cannot believe I got the starring role!

    A declarative sentence   **C** imperative sentence
    B exclamatory sentence   **D** interrogative sentence

Varying Sentences in Your Writing

Good writers use different kinds of sentences to add emphasis to their writing.

- Did you know that I am taking acting lessons? Acting is hard! I want to be in the school play. Tell me what role I should study for.

A Choose the strongest sentence from the box to end this persuasive paragraph. Add end punctuation to the sentences and write the paragraph.

> I have to be in the play this year too.
> Please consider casting me in the starring role.
> If I play a pickle well, I can handle any role!

1. I believe that my acting experience qualifies me for the lead role in the annual town play ___ **2.** Did you see me in last year's production of *Penny's Pickle* ___ **3.** I played the pickle ___ **4.** What a great performance it was ___ **5.** Have you ever seen a more realistic portrayal of a pickle ___ **6.** _____

B Correct the capitalization and end punctuation in each sentence. Add an opening interrogative sentence and a closing exclamatory sentence. Write the paragraph.

7. _____ **8.** tryouts for the community chorus will be tomorrow night **9.** they are being held at the movie theater downtown **10.** i'll take the bus there **11.** could you pick me up afterward **12.** i know that you are busy, but it is very important to me **13.** please pick me up at 8:30 **14.** _____

C Write a short persuasive argument to convince an adult to let you do something creative, such as acting or joining the school band. Vary the types of sentences you use to add impact to your writing.

Capitalization

· ·

Use a **capital letter** to begin a sentence.

- **T**he little boy shrieked when he saw the bug.

Capitalize the first word and every important word of a **proper noun.**
Proper nouns name particular persons, places, or things.

- **D**avid went to **C**osta **R**ica to study bugs.

Capitalize the first word and every important word of a **title.**

- He wrote a book called ***B**ugs, **B**ugs, and **M**ore **B**ugs: **U**gh!*

Capitalize the first letter of an **abbreviation.** Many abbreviations end
in a period. Capitalize both letters in the abbreviation of a state name for
a mailing address, but do not use a period.

- 4234 **W**. Canyon **D**r.   Las Vegas, **NV**

Capitalize **days of the week** and **months of the year.**

- The museum is closed on **M**ondays in **J**une.

Capitalize **titles** before people's names. Some titles may also be abbreviations.

- **D**r. Samuelson   **M**rs. Arvida Jones   **S**enator Jiménez

· ·

 A Rewrite each sentence using correct capitalization.

1. matthew goes to martin luther king, jr., high school in chicago.
2. his class took a trip last friday.
3. the students visited the field museum.
4. the museum guide, dr. starr, showed matthew's class the insect exhibit.
5. the class learned about insects that come from asia and africa.
6. students viewed a film called *the secret life of bugs.*
7. matthew bought a postcard to send to aunt judy in toronto.
8. aunt judy is an artist who has paintings in the ontario museum.

B Write **C** if the group of words is capitalized correctly. If the group of words is capitalized incorrectly, rewrite it using correct capitalization.

1. hudson River
2. Kentucky Derby
3. the fourth of july
4. Philadelphia, Pennsylvania
5. capt. Jerry smart
6. Antelope, tx 76350
7. Friday, April 16, 2005
8. general Ulysses s. grant
9. Marc e. smith, jr.
10. dr. valenzuela

C Correct the capitalization in the following letter. Write the letter.

june 14, 2005

Dear dr. starr,

thank you for showing my class the *world of insects* exhibit at the field museum last friday. we enjoyed meeting you and your assistant, ms. harris. I especially enjoyed learning about the beetles and the grasshoppers. when I am older, I would like to attend the university of chicago. I hope to follow in your footsteps and become a doctor. thank you again for showing us around.

Sincerely,
oscar grant

Review and Assess

Rewrite each sentence using correct capitalization.

1. last night, I went to a restaurant on south boulevard.
2. the restaurant is owned by my neighbor, mr. Gupta.
3. he has written a cookbook titled *curry Up and Cook.*
4. the book is sold at Cookbooks for all on state Street.
5. every august he returns home to Goma, india, to collect recipes.
6. tuesday, mr. gupta will cook dinner for my dad and me.
7. i will ask him to autograph a copy of his book for my friend ana.
8. ana lives on main street in west newton.
9. She has cookbooks from france, india, and italy.

Read the following groups of words. Write the letter of the group of words that is correct.

10. **A** mr. gonzalez   **C** Mr. Gonzalez
    B Mr. gonzalez   **D** mr. Gonzalez

11. **A** Wednesday, January 7   **C** Wednesday, january 7
    B wednesday, January 7   **D** wednesday, january 7

12. **A** Sgt. spitz   **C** sgt. Spitz
    B sgt. spitz   **D** Sgt. Spitz

13. **A** Palo Alto, CA 90002   **C** palo Alto, CA 90002
    B Palo alto, CA 90002   **D** Palo Alto, Ca 90002

14. **A** paris, France   **C** Paris, france
    B Paris, France   **D** paris, france

15. **A** the film *star wars*   **C** the Film *star wars*
    B the film *Star wars*   **D** the film *Star Wars*

16. **A** dr. terry jones   **C** Dr. terry jones
    B Dr. Terry Jones   **D** dr. Terry jones

Observing the Rules for Capitalization

Pay attention to the rules for capitalization in your writing. Make sure words are capitalized correctly so your readers are not confused.

A Match the letter of the capitalization rule with each mistake in the paragraph below.

> **A** Capitalize the first letter of a sentence.
> **B** Capitalize proper nouns that name places.
> **C** Capitalize titles before people's names.
> **D** Capitalize proper nouns that name people.

1. We are having a party for dr. Celsey Lane. **2.** her book about insects was just published. **3.** The bookstore in jacksonville has many copies. **4.** I ordered one from the store owner, eileen horan.

B Correct the capitalization in the sentences of this letter. Write a closing sentence. Add a date, greeting, closing, and signature. Write the letter.

5. yesterday we went to the Museum of bizarre bugs. **6.** Have you ever been there, jenny? **7.** I think you should go when you get back from camp silverlake. **8.** you will love the show because there are so many interesting bugs! **9.** I have arranged with the director, dr. Gramercy, to give you a tour. **10.** _____

C Write a short letter or note to convince a friend to do something interesting. Include a date, greeting, closing, and signature. Be sure to use correct capitalization.

Commas

A **series** is a list of three or more items. Items may be words (such as nouns, adjectives, or verbs) or phrases (such as prepositional phrases). Use **commas** to separate the items in a series. A comma is used after each item in the series except the last.

> Gina ate chicken, rice, and beans.

> Her meal was healthful, satisfying, and delicious.

> After lunch she went for a walk, bought a newspaper, and sat in the park.

> Then she went down the street, under a bridge, and over the walkway.

Commas are also used to set off the names of people who are **directly addressed,** or spoken to. Use two commas if the name is in the middle of a sentence.

> Guadalupe, may I have some tortillas?

> No, Rafael, wait until dinner time.

> Then you can eat all you want, Rafael.

Commas usually follow **introductory words** in sentences.

> Suddenly, she spotted her friend Mick.

 A Read each sentence. Write **C** if commas are used correctly. Write **NC** if they are not used correctly. Then correct each sentence.

1. Folk tales are written to entertain amuse, or inform.
2. Harry, what is your favorite folk tale?
3. Actually I don't know any folk tales.
4. My aunt reads folk tales poems, and other stories to children.
5. Have you heard her read, Jerry?
6. Her favorite story has talking pigs, goats, and walruses.
7. I think I read that one Marci.

B Write the sentences. Add commas to complete each sentence.

1. Do you like spicy food Lyle?
2. Yes I really like foods with a lot of flavor.
3. Would you like to come for dinner Lyle?
4. My dad is a great cook Lyle and his specialty is Mexican food.
5. Thank you José I really look forward to coming over.
6. I am free on Saturday José.
7. You will meet my family eat a tasty meal and have a great time.
8. I will ask my dad to make tortillas salsa and shrimp.
9. At last I will have an authentic Mexican meal!

C Choose a word or group of words from the box to complete each sentence. Add commas as needed. Write the sentences.

> spicy fresh and delicious   María   Mexico City
> down the street behind the theater and near the school
> yes   wheat rice and corn

10. I eat _____ at most meals.
11. Tell me _____ where do you like to eat?
12. Dana, my favorite restaurant is in _____.
13. The food there is _____.
14. _____ I've eaten there also.
15. It is located _____.

Review and Assess

Add commas as needed in each sentence. Write the sentences.

1. Aaron what is your favorite kind of food?
2. I adore Italian food because it is healthful fresh and tasty.
3. Paolo have you ever been to Italy?
4. No but I would like to go there one day.
5. Would you like to go there with me next year Paolo?
6. Yes I'd love to go on vacation with you.
7. We could visit Rome Florence and Venice.
8. That sounds like a wonderful trip Aaron.

Write the letter of the phrase that uses commas correctly to complete each sentence.

9. _____ was born on April 27, 1963.

   A Yes my mother   C Yes, my mother
   B Yes my, mother   D Yes my mother,

10. She grew up in Rapid City, Iowa _____ and has lived there all her life.

    A Tanya   C Tanya,
    B , Tanya,   D ,Tanya

11. She loves to read plays, _____.

    A poems and novels   C poems, and, novels
    B poems, and novels   D poems and, novels

12. I would like you to _____ because she is a special person.

    A meet her, Amy   C meet her Amy,
    B meet her Amy   D meet her, Amy,

13. _____ me funny stories.

    A Frequently, she tells   C Frequently she tells
    B Frequently, she, tells   D Frequently she, tells

Making Your Writing Clear with Commas

Commas make your writing easier to read. Commas can also be used to strengthen your persuasive argument. Use commas to set off your strongest statements with introductory words and phrases such as *most importantly* and *clearly*.

A   Write the letter that matches the mistake in each sentence.

    A   Use commas to separate items in a series.

    B   Use commas with a name in direct address.

    C   Use commas to follow introductory phrases.

    1. The International Food Fair will be open next Wednesday Thursday and Friday.   **2.** Yes this year the fair will take place in Tarzana, California.   **3.** I think we should take a field trip to the fair to learn about the foods people eat in countries such as Italy Hungary and Ethiopia.   **4.** Mr. Hanford I am sure we will all enjoy tasting a variety of yummy foods.   **5.** Without a doubt our class will learn a lot and have a great time!

B   Add commas as needed to the sentences below. Then write an opening sentence and a closing sentence to complete the persuasive paragraph. Write the paragraph.

    6. I would like to learn more about Mexican food customs and traditions.   **7.** Actually the exhibition begins on Monday.   **8.** I suppose Mrs. Kim our class would visit the exhibit on a weekend day so that we do not miss any school.   **9.** Of course I would be happy to make all the arrangements.   **10.** Clearly the exhibit fits well with what we have studied so far this year.

C   Think of a field trip your class might enjoy. Write a letter to persuade your teacher to take your class on the field trip. Be sure to use commas correctly.

Quotations and Quotation Marks

A person's exact words are a **direct quotation.** Direct quotations begin with capital letters and end with proper punctuation marks. Use **quotation marks** (" ") at the beginning and end of the speaker's exact words.

> Jim said, "I like going to the movies."

If the quotation comes first in a sentence, use a comma, a question mark, or an exclamation mark to separate the quotation from the rest of the sentence.

> "That was the best movie I ever saw!" exclaimed Dalia.

If the quotation comes last in a sentence, use a comma to separate it from the rest of the sentence: Mira asked, "Can we see it again?"

Sometimes words that tell who is speaking may interrupt a direct quotation. Then two sets of quotation marks are used. The words that tell who is speaking may be followed by a comma or end punctuation. Use a comma if the second part of the quotation does not begin a new sentence. Use end punctuation and a capital letter if it does.

> "I'd like to see a comedy," I offered, "but an action film is fine."
>
> "I prefer action movies," Jim replied. "What's playing?"

Put commas and end punctuation inside the last quotation marks.

> "I'd like some popcorn," she said. "Have you seen this movie?" Tina asked.

 A Write **C** if quotation marks are used correctly in each sentence. Write **NC** if quotation marks are used incorrectly.

1. "Let me show you the photographs from my trip," offered Ben.
2. "This one is all black," said Bernie. "Was your camera broken?"
3. "Not at all, Ben replied. "I took that photo at night."

B Add quotation marks to each sentence. Write the new sentences.

1. Did you go to school today? inquired Malik.
2. Of course, John replied, I always go to school.
3. Malik asked, But didn't you realize today was a holiday?
4. No wonder nobody was there! John exclaimed.
5. He added, I'm always doing silly things.
6. Sometimes I put on two different colored socks, John admitted.
7. We all make mistakes, Malik suggested. I make plenty myself.
8. I wish everyone was so understanding, John sighed.
9. Well, Malik responded, that's what friends are for.
10. Let's go to a movie! they shouted to each other.

C Write each sentence correctly. Add quotation marks, capital letters, and correct punctuation.

11. what is your name asked the girl
12. my name is Max he answered
13. do you enjoy drawing she inquired
14. Max shouted I love drawing
15. the girl admitted I'm a terrible artist
16. I enjoy it anyway she added
17. have you thought of taking lessons Max suggested
18. that's a great idea the girl said

Review and Assess

Add quotation marks to each sentence. Write the new sentences.

1. Let's listen to some music, Franklin suggested.
2. How are your CDs organized? he asked.
3. Organized? What do you mean? I replied.
4. Are they in alphabetical order? Franklin inquired.
5. They aren't in any order at all! I admitted.

Write the letter of the answer that completes each sentence correctly.

6. "Did you go to the concert last _____ asked Don.

   A night,"   C night?"
   B night"   D night"?

7. _____ Rita responded. "Was it fun?"

   A "No,"   C "No,
   B "No"   D "No."

8. "I've never heard such screeching _____ Don complained.

   A noises"   C noises
   B noises,"   D noises?"

9. "My ears are still _____ he added.

   A ringing"   C ringing
   B ringing,"   D ringing",

10. Rita said in _____ terrible."

   A sympathy "That's   C sympathy, "That's
   B sympathy, "That's"   D sympathy, That's

Using Quotations to Support Your Opinions

Good writers often support their persuasive arguments with quotations. They use quotations from sources such as books, articles, or interviews they conduct with experts.

A Add two sentences from the list that support the ideas in the paragraph. Write the sentences with quotation marks and correct punctuation.

He said You're a smart guy.

Read the longest article first he said.

Start with the article or book that looks most enjoyable she wrote.

1. I had so many articles to read for my report. **2.** My dad does research all the time, so I asked him for advice. **3.** _____ **4.** I still felt overwhelmed! **5.** Then I remembered a quote from *Being a Better Student* by Shari Lamott. **6.** _____ **7.** I decided to take her advice. **8.** Wouldn't you do the same?

B Add quotation marks and correct punctuation to the sentences. Replace the verb *said* with verbs such as *replied, observed, added, complained,* and *shouted*. Write the paragraph.

9. That lot has been sitting empty for too many years said Mrs. Marvel. **10.** She said I wish somebody would clean it out. **11.** I have an idea I said Why don't we turn it into a vegetable garden? **12.** I asked my neighbors to contribute supplies, and many of them said Sure! **13.** A wise person once said There's no time like the present!

C Write a speech to persuade your schoolmates to help improve something at your school. Conduct interviews to gather quotations to support your argument.

Review of Compound and Complex Sentences

You can make your writing more interesting by varying your sentences.
A **simple sentence** contains one complete subject and one complete predicate.
A **compound sentence** is two simple sentences with related ideas joined with
a comma and a conjunction such as *and, but,* or *or.*
A **complex sentence** is a simple sentence combined with a group of words
that cannot stand alone. The group of words has a subject and a predicate. It
is joined to the sentence with a word such as *if, because, as,* or *when.*

Simple sentences: I adore sculpture. My sister prefers painting.

Compound sentence: She takes painting classes, and she is very talented.

Complex sentence: When I look at her paintings, I am quite impressed.

 A Read each sentence. Write whether each sentence is **simple, compound,**
or **complex.**

1. The sculptures of Alexander Calder are fascinating to me.
2. Some of his works are found in public places, but other works are kept
   in private homes.
3. Many of Calder's sculptures move, and some of them
   make noise.
4. When painters view his work, they are often inspired.
5. Children like his sculptures because they are colorful.
6. Calder's work was always popular, and it will remain popular for
   a long time.
7. If you get a chance to see his sculptures, take photographs of them
   from different angles.

B Join the two simple sentences to form a compound sentence. Use a comma and *or, and,* or *but* to combine them. Write the new sentences.

1. Art can be hard to understand. It is worth the effort.
2. You can view art at a museum. You can make it yourself.
3. Some art shows real things. Some art springs from the imagination.
4. Many artists live in cities. Some artists prefer the countryside.
5. The artist Monet painted flowers. He also painted haystacks.
6. Degas painted dancers. They are extremely beautiful.
7. Do you like Monet? Do you prefer Degas?
8. I enjoy Monet's paintings. Morandi is my favorite artist.
9. Morandi painted pictures of bottles. He painted fruit as well.
10. His paintings can make you feel sad. They can inspire you.

C Add a simple sentence to each group of words to form a compound or a complex sentence. Write the new sentences with correct punctuation.

11. _____ because I am so interested in art.
12. I appreciate fine paintings, _____.
13. Some drawings are easy to understand, _____.
14. When I look at a beautiful painting, _____.
15. _____, but I have never been to the Museum of Modern Art.
16. If it is a miserable, rainy day, _____.
17. I go to the museum often, _____.
18. When I grow up, _____.

Review and Assess

Write **simple**, **compound**, or **complex** to identify each sentence.

1. The pupil of your eye looks like a tiny black dot, but it is really a hole. **2.** Your irises contract in bright light, and your pupils get smaller. **3.** This is a good thing because too much light can damage the retina. **4.** Many people are near-sighted. **5.** If you are near-sighted, you might ask your doctor about laser surgery.

Write the letter of the word you would use to complete each sentence.

6. The most important tools that artists have are their eyes, _____ musicians are more dependent on their ears. **7.** _____ people listen to music, they often close their eyes. **8.** Many artists and musicians enjoy each other's work, _____ sometimes they work together. **9.** A few artists are even musicians as well, _____ at least they try to be musicians. **10.** _____ long as we have artists and musicians, our lives will continue to be full.

6. A if   **C** or
    B but   **D** when

7. A Or   **C** Because
    B But   **D** When

8. A and   **C** when
    B as if   **D** as

9. A and   **C** or
    B because   **D** but

10. A As   **C** And
     B If   **D** But

Varying Sentences to Improve Style

Enrich your writing style by including compound and complex sentences. You can combine short, choppy sentences to make your writing smoother and more interesting.

- It has bright colors. I really like that painting.
  We could hang it on our bulletin board. We can put it on the door.

- Because it has bright colors, I really like that painting.
  We could hang it on our bulletin board, or we can put it on the door.

A Combine each pair of sentences using the word in ( ). Remember to add a comma. Write the paragraph.

1. Trophies and posters are important. I think having beautiful art to look at is just as important. (but) **2.** We want to make our halls more cheerful. We should hang pictures there. (If) **3.** We could make space for art on the third floor. We could display it near the school entrance. (or) **4.** The entrance might be the best place to put the art. Visitors would get a nice first impression. (so) **5.** People see art all around them. They feel they are living in a happy, creative place. (When)

B Complete the sentences below by making them compound or complex sentences. Then write one complex sentence and one compound sentence of your own to finish the paragraph. Write the persuasive paragraph.

6. When I look at a painting, _____. **7.** Some paintings are very complex, _____. **8.** _____, I suggest we organize a field trip to the local art museum. **9.** We can arrange to go on a tour, _____. **10.** The museum is free to everyone on Wednesday evenings, _____. **11.** _____ **12.** _____

C Write a paragraph about your favorite painting or song. Explain why you think it is special. Use compound and complex sentences to enrich your writing style.

Writing a Persuasive Argument

A **test** may ask you to write a persuasive argument. Support your ideas with examples, facts, reasons, and words and phrases such as *should* and *most important*. Follow the tips below.

Understand the prompt. Make sure you know what to do. Read the prompt carefully. A prompt for a persuasive argument could look like this:

> **What issues are important to you in school? What would improve your school? Write a persuasive argument that you might use to convince your teacher or principal to make a change in your school.**

Key words and phrases are *issues, improve, persuasive argument,* and *convince.*

Find a good topic. Find something you feel strongly about. Be sure you can think of enough good reasons to support your opinion.

Organize your ideas. Write a persuasive-argument organizer. Use the organizer to write your opinion and to list reasons that support your opinion.

Persuasive Argument: Works of art at school would help everyone work better.
Reasons:
• They would make the hallways brighter.   • Paintings teach us about history and the way people dressed and lived.   • We would be more eager to learn.   • Everyone would be more relaxed.   • When the building looks better, people are happier to be there.   • Plain walls or student drawings are dull.

Write a good beginning. Write an opening sentence that grabs the reader's attention and clearly states your opinion.

Develop and elaborate ideas. Use your organizer to focus your writing on the topic. Use powerful words to persuade your readers.

Write a strong ending. Let the ending sum up your opinion. You may want to save your strongest reason for the end.

Check your work. Share your work with a classmate to get suggestions about making your writing more interesting and persuasive.

See how the persuasive argument below addresses the prompt, has a strong beginning and end, and stays focused on the topic.

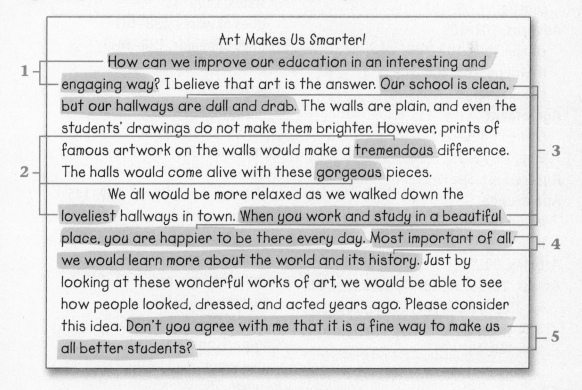

Art Makes Us Smarter!

1 — How can we improve our education in an interesting and engaging way? I believe that art is the answer. Our school is clean, but our hallways are dull and drab. The walls are plain, and even the students' drawings do not make them brighter. However, prints of famous artwork on the walls would make a tremendous difference. — 3

2 — The halls would come alive with these gorgeous pieces.

We all would be more relaxed as we walked down the loveliest hallways in town. When you work and study in a beautiful place, you are happier to be there every day. Most important of all, — 4
we would learn more about the world and its history. Just by looking at these wonderful works of art, we would be able to see how people looked, dressed, and acted years ago. Please consider this idea. Don't you agree with me that it is a fine way to make us — 5
all better students?

1. An opening question attracts the reader's attention.
2. The writer uses persuasive words effectively.
3. Compound and complex sentences add variety.
4. The argument builds to the most important reason.
5. This strong ending sums up the topic and the writer's thoughts.

INDEX

S

T

V

W

Web, 66

Word choice. *See* Writing.

Writing

Art Acknowledgments

Yvette Santiago Banek 96, 103, 107, 118, 129, 130 Paula Becker 33, 47
Rose Mary Berlin 27, 73, 74, 85 Franklin Hammond 17, 22, 56, 68, 77, 104, 113, 125
Ronnie Rooney 20, 41, 55, 81, 92, 108, 143